Call and Response

CALL AND RESPONSE

10 Leadership Lessons from the Black Church

L. MICHELLE SMITH
Note from Viola Davis

AMISTAD
An Imprint of HarperCollinsPublishers

Excerpt from *The Black Church: This Is Our Story, This Is Our Song* by Henry Louis Gates, Jr., copyright © 2021 by Henry Louis Gates, Jr. Used by permission of Penguin Press, an imprint of Penguin Publishing Group, a division of Penguin Random House LLC. All rights reserved.

Excerpt from the *Holy Bible, New Living Translation*, copyright © 1996, 2004, 2015 by Tyndale House Foundation. Used by permission of Tyndale House Publishers Inc., Carol Stream, Illinois 60188. All rights reserved.

Without limiting the exclusive rights of any author, contributor or the publisher of this publication, any unauthorized use of this publication to train generative artificial intelligence (AI) technologies is expressly prohibited. HarperCollins also exercise their rights under Article 4(3) of the Digital Single Market Directive 2019/790 and expressly reserve this publication from the text and data mining exception.

CALL AND RESPONSE. Copyright © 2026 by L. Michelle Smith. Note copyright © 2026 by Viola Davis. All rights reserved. No part of this book may be used or reproduced in any manner whatsoever without written permission except in the case of brief quotations embodied in critical articles and reviews. For information, address HarperCollins Publishers, 195 Broadway, New York, NY 10007. In Europe, HarperCollins Publishers, Macken House, 39/40 Mayor Street Upper, Dublin 1, D01 C9W8, Ireland.

HarperCollins books may be purchased for educational, business, or sales promotional use. For information, please email the Special Markets Department at SPsales@harpercollins.com.

harpercollins.com

FIRST EDITION

Designed by Jason Kayser

Library of Congress Cataloging-in-Publication Data has been applied for.

ISBN 978-0-06-342593-4

Printed in the United States of America

25 26 27 28 29 LBC 5 4 3 2 1

In memory of Dr. Caesar Arthur Walter Clark (1914–2008), "Little Caesar," "The Preacher's Preacher," a giant among men. You led with courage, resilience, an entrepreneurial spirit, and eloquence as an amazing pastor, friend, and visionary.

CALL-AND-RESPONSE exchanges between congregation and pastor; at its best, the seamless interplay between the rhythms of the sermon and the harmonies of song, both reflecting the pastor's biblical exegesis of "the text for today"; modes of prayer, both formal and informal; and possession by the omnipresent Holy Spirit: all are really links in a chain of cultural continuity that connects Africa to Black America. They are repetitions with brilliantly improvised differences within a received "frame," a discursive frame, a sacred cultural "language" in which worshippers are so thoroughly fluent and literate that they can riff within that frame freely and creatively. They are echoes of sermonic and musical formations of the past fashioned by our ancestors over successive generations of creation, repetition, revision, and, most importantly, improvisation, quite probably since the first hundred years of American slavery.

We see it in jazz, with musicians riffing upon standards in the jazz tradition and in popular culture. John Coltrane did it with "My Favorite Things," and Louis Armstrong did it with "La Vie en Rose," to take just two of countless examples. We see it in the work of performers today, this living chain of Black cultural signifiers imbibed and internalized, respectfully acknowledged yet sublimely transformed. Daring and defiant artists, ranging from Thomas A. Dorsey, with his experiments in gospel, to Kirk Franklin, with his fresh fusions of hymns with hip-hop, risked the opprobrium of the more conservative keepers of the tradition by daring to alter and infuse the sacred with borrowed techniques from the scandalously secular: that long and controversial tradition of Saturday night sneaking into the church on Sunday morning. With a language all its own, symbols all its own, the Black church offered a reprieve from the racist world...

—Dr. Henry Louis Gates Jr., *The Black Church: This Is Our Story, This Is Our Song*

Contents

Foreword and Note from Viola Davis xi

Preface xiii

Introduction 1

1 **Faith and Purpose:** A Child Will Lead Them 15

2 **Community:** The Covenant and Circle Unbroken 31

3 **Speaking:** The Power of Storytelling and Performance 53

4 **Resilience:** A Balm for the Burden 71

5 **Perseverance:** Learning to Keep on Keeping On 93

6 **Collaboration:** Leadership in a Song 113

7 **Accountability:** Keeping It Righteous 135

8 **Social Justice:** A Legacy of Overcoming 151

9 **Creativity and Innovation:** Miracles and Blessings 179

10 **Economic Empowerment:** Building Kingdoms 195

The Invitation: A Letter to Leaders 217

The Coaching Guide: Thirty-Eight Powerful Questions Based on the Ten Lessons to Usher You to Extraordinary Leadership 229

Acknowledgments 237

Resources 245

Bibliography 255

Foreword and Note from Viola Davis

Call and Response is published by Amistad in collaboration with JVL Media, a full-service independent publisher and media packaging firm, founded by Viola Davis, Julius Tennon, and Lavaille Lavette. The company is dedicated to delivering exceptional literature that celebrates and amplifies a diverse range of voices and experiences. In addition to its independent projects, JVL collaborates with leading publishing and media entities to curate and deliver an eclectic spectrum of high-caliber literature. By championing inclusivity and innovation, JVL Media aims to inspire, enlighten, and entertain readers worldwide.

"This endeavor embodies our collective aspiration—to champion and elevate voices that resonate with authenticity and are often overlooked. Our mission is to interlace a rich mosaic of both fiction and nonfiction that not only stirs the imagination but also venerates the enduring heritage of storytellers from diverse walks of life," says Davis.

Dear Reader,
"Call and Response" is a powerful work that honors the legacy of the Black church while offering a bold, fresh vision for the future

of leadership. With insight and clarity, L. Michelle Smith shows how faith, resilience, and innovation can guide us through today's challenges and prepare the next generation of leaders.

What makes this book extraordinary is the way it bridges history and progress—it is both a tribute to the strength that carried us here and a roadmap for where we must go next. In these uncertain times, "Call and Response" provides wisdom, inspiration, and direction.

It is a book I believe everyone should read.

Preface

Music is very much a part of my DNA. I was born hardwired to sing it, play it, listen to it, survey it, judge it, dissect it, appreciate it, dance and bop to it. I love hip-hop, but I'm also churchy. I love gospel music too and am a huge fan of history and a student of culture. That means that Dr. Henry Louis Gates Jr.'s work is my cup of tea because he often centers the music of Black folk. Within the past nine years, I've been blessed to call him friend after meeting and working together on a few projects. And I was incredibly excited when he executive produced and hosted a documentary and live show on PBS called *Gospel*. Gospel music is a genre of music that sprang from the Black church tradition and is built on the chassis of the call and response.

At the beginning of the documentary, Dr. Gates talks about his fascination with the way the Black Church conflates singing with preaching. In fact, later in the series, gospel legend Shirley Caesar articulates it best when she says that the preachers sing and the singers preach. It's so true. So when you consider that singing is simply sustained speech, it follows that a preacher who is really into his or her message may stretch a word or two or an exclamation into something that might sound musical—not to mention "whooping," where the preacher begins to elongate his words into a melody or riff, repeatedly singing what he's saying in only about three, four, or five notes; or "tuning," where the organist plays the Hammond organ to answer the preacher's call.

Singers might also, in the midst of a song, sound like they are speaking—or perhaps they do exhort within the notes and bars. Caesar herself "got sat down" in her own church early on for that because back then, most churches frowned upon women preachers, as some still do today. If you ask most Black churchgoers where the ritual of the call and response originated, they'd likely say the pulpits of many Black churches. However, the practice actually originated in our music, long, long ago.

Research reveals that the call and response can be traced all the way back to the songs of sub-Saharan Africa. It made its way to the United States and other parts of the world no thanks to the transatlantic slave trade. It became a staple in the work songs and spirituals of enslaved Black people. Eventually, it seeped into the churches when freedmen were able to build their own, and soon thereafter, it could be heard in popular music and still is today.

What is it, exactly? It's where one person, the leader, sings one line, and others, the chorus or congregation, answer with more singing—most often the same words or notes or an actual answer to whatever the sentiment raised. Since so much of the traditional Black worship experience fuses singing and storytelling, it was a natural evolution for the call and response to find its way into the pulpit. Whether in preaching or in singing, someone leads with a few bars or a few words, and the congregation or the chorus answers with a few words, a few bars, or in some cases a shout. To this day, you will hear this tradition reflected in everything from contemporary music to even political speeches, most notably from Black candidates, and even former First Ladies. Who remembers Michelle Obama taking us to church at the 2024 Democratic National Convention with *"Do something!"*?

In fact, in one part of the book, I discuss how the practice can even be noted in rap music as early as Kurtis Blow, the first commercially successful rapper. He is also an ordained minister. Remember "The Breaks"? That song includes a call and response. The DJ managing his cuts "on the ones and twos," a very young Joseph "Rev Run" Simmons. I personally believe that preachers and rappers are twins, separated at birth, two sides of the same coin—except in the case of Kurtis Blow, Rev Run, Hammer, Mase, Lecrae, Trip Lee, and Kirk Franklin, who all happen to be one in the same.

Wherever you hear the call and response today, or even back in the day, there is always a leader and there are always followers. Seems a book about leadership where I explore the lessons from a cultural institution like the Black Church should be called something relevant to that culture. What better way to honor and shout out everyone from whooping preachers to gutbucket gospel singers, leaders you experience first in the Black Church, than with a reference to a ritual core to the traditions.

I also reference research from neuroscience and positive psychology throughout this book, and it is my intention to show that something that is so spiritual, so emotional, even a little regular and sometimes old-fashioned is actually cerebral and scientific. You will find that the call and response is itself a happiness trigger—sparking a neurological joy-cocktail of hormones in the brain that bonds us in a way that promotes everything from well-being to resilience to success despite the odds. All of this allows us to get big things done in business and the community, as a group and as individuals.

So, in the case of this business leadership book, call and response is not only a tool for success. It is a metaphor. It is also my way of leading a conversation, a full-on discourse about an important topic that I will be encouraging a response to, by business leaders, especially in the corporate realm, and church leaders too.

There's a leadership pipeline from the pews, but it isn't as robust as it once was due to several factors that I uncover along the way.

What will you do about it?

That's the call.

After reading this book, I'll listen for your response.

Introduction

The holiday break had come, and my daughter and I parked ourselves in the family room at my parents' house. I was snuggled up in warm sweats, taking up most of the sofa as I dozed, slipping in and out of consciousness. It was drizzling outside, and my daughter had engaged my father in a game of checkers, sprawled out on the floor. I'd put work behind me for the next few weeks, and I was more than happy to rest after months on months of speaking across the country and facilitating workshops, supporting executives in their quest for better leadership, and simply being a mom. My private executive and personal coaching practice was thriving, and it was time for a much-needed break.

Just as I was about to drift off to sleep again, my mother emerged from the back room. She eased up to me, wearing her signature robe and headscarf, a signal that she was ready to turn in. She didn't speak. She simply handed me a well-preserved black-and-white photo. I examined the picture, and with a sudden burst of enthusiasm, I jumped up and asked, "How could you hand me this so calmly?! Where did this come from? I've got so many questions!"

Her answer was shockingly delivered with an ultra-calm tone.

She seemed so unfazed to have something of such historical significance in her hand.

"Someone just gave it to me at the church," she said. "I'm not sure who. James, do you remember?" Daddy just looked over and shrugged. How could they be so unimpressed? I was still stunned when my daughter started to chime in.

"What is it, Mommy?! What is it?!" I called her over to see and asked, "Who is that standing in the middle?"

I knew she would know because she had studied about him since the age of three. Back then, she called him "Martin Looper King, Junior." She could pronounce it a little better at the age of eight.

"You wouldn't remember him, though," I told her as I pointed to the other man in the photo, standing on the end. "That's a very young C. A. W. Clark. He was the pastor at Good Street Baptist Church when I was growing up. He had passed away by the time you were born," I told my daughter. My mother was still standing in complete calmness as I recognized several of my friends' grandmothers in the photo, likely in their twenties in the picture. It was apparent what was happening. The group had just finished preparing a meal for the congregation in honor of their guest, and as the story goes, that guest only made four trips to the Dallas–Fort Worth area in his short lifetime, and this one almost didn't happen.

My mother recounted a story shared with her by elders in the church. My parents weren't members back then. In fact, they were still high school students at that time. They say the year was 1959, and just as the young civil rights leader was beginning to emerge as a central figure to the movement, he planned a trip to the area. The only problem was that most Black pastors were too afraid to host him for fear of retaliation from angry white supremacists, still terrorizing the South by bombing churches. Everyone, that is, except Pastor Clark. He too was only just emerging as the powerful figure that he would ultimately become in the Black Church. He displayed unwavering courage and resilience and openly invited the young civil rights leader to his pulpit. That story blew me away, and it inspired a thought: "That was an example of true leadership," I said to my family. They agreed, and it explained so much about what I had experienced as a child and through my young adult years at that very church.

I wasn't born when the photo was taken. I would arrive many years later, but it was at that point in my parents' den that I would begin to ponder what it was like for me "growing up Good Street," what some called the original megachurch with its one-thousand-plus membership, and how many other Black business leaders had similar experiences at various churches throughout the country, had similar stories to tell, saw similar examples of resilient leadership grounded in faith and purpose.

That my nearly-eighty-year-old parents were there holding on to a piece of history that not only defined the church's history but punctuated such a crucial time in our Black heritage was stirring, inspiring, and stunning all at once. I surmise that they were so calm and unaffected because they lived through Jim Crow and the Civil Rights Movement. Stories about a young King and even Jesse Jackson were common for them. In fact, they would hold new insights for me because they lived through King's assassination and other historical moments. But these leadership lessons and leadership icons in what I coined "Black America's original social network," the Black Church, were all around us, and more than close to home—it was in our home. I too took for granted that Aretha Franklin visited my church in Dallas to attend the funeral of blues singer Johnnie Taylor and later Pastor Clark's because Clark was a friend and contemporary of her father, Rev. C. L. Franklin. That I could grab candy from Pastor Clark's office while my dad mic'd up Rev. Jesse Jackson, even before his historic run for the US presidency, still blows my mind today. I heard Charley Pride sing more than one hymn from the same choir stand where I sang solos as a little girl and a young adult. It wasn't simply that the pews and pulpit were dripping with leaders whether celebrities, educators, business owners, lawmakers, doctors and nurses, attorneys and judges. It was that these people were living examples of leadership in every field they represented, and that excellence was something that they not only learned but cultivated right there in the Black Church while we looked on. We were surrounded by them and their testimonies. They taught us by example, through proximity and in practice, that resilience, faith and purpose, perseverance, community, social justice, creativity and innovation, accountability, storytelling and teaching and collaboration, and more were core to their success. Those lessons were also core to the success of the Black community at large, including those who would eventually find themselves in the halls and towers of some of the largest organizations in our nation.

What other leadership lessons had I and others learned in the Black Church? I wanted to know the direct impact of the Black Church on business leaders like me and how we might be carrying these lessons into the strongholds of corporate America, from the pews to the pipeline. I wanted to know how these lessons benefited us and how we can intentionally begin to recognize and foster them generation over generation.

That black-and-white photo was only one turning point for me. The second came after I concluded a keynote address that garnered twenty-five million social media impressions online in real time after a forty-five-minute talk with only roughly 150 people in the audience. Someone asked me, "Where did you learn to speak like that?" I initially replied that I was a media and communications trainer for C-level executives, preparing them for appearances on big stages and national news shows. After those words streamed from my lips, nearly reflexively, I sat and thought for a moment. That wasn't right. The truth was that when you were promoted to the high school class at my church, you were thrust in front of an adult Sunday School class once a month to teach. After, you were in a rotation to present the highlights of the lesson to the entire Sunday School body when reconvening. I also had a front-row seat (and sometimes a backstage one too) to witness an all-star lineup of some of the best preachers in the country as they whipped the congregation into a frenzy on nearly every Sunday morning; I had been placed behind a microphone to shift minds, hearts, and the atmosphere, either while singing or speaking. From then on, I would answer that question differently, giving credit where credit was due.

That photo of King was also a reminder of how valuable yet ethereal the traditions of the traditional Black Church actually are. As I looked at the photo and saw these young women in their pencil skirts and dresses, all white, with corsages, well-coiffed hair, and pointy-toed black pumps, it occurred to me that the general shift away from church attendance in the United States was compounded by the unprecedented pandemic lockdown. Additionally, the more modern approaches to services, worship, and even after-service activities could cause us to lose a grip on a cultural tradition that offered us so much leadership enrichment and culture all at once. Yes, even the well-choreographed and extravagant after-church dinners and dinners on the ground impacted the way many Black leaders see the world and their work today. Looking back on the way it was, for so many of today's Black leaders so much of the leadership lessons and modeling happened in person at the church and in the community.

The Leadership Lessons

On my quest to learn if my experience was similar to other Black leaders at the highest levels of business, I developed a survey that probed into their experiences with the Black Church. I asked how it had or hadn't influenced them, if they had experiences as children and how that informed their approach to business, and if they had children, whether they would want a similar experience for them. I also wanted to know how other external factors might be affecting that experience for themselves and their children. More than 82 percent of the survey respondents said that they attended a Black church either a great deal or a lot during their lifetime, and 76 percent of respondents attribute their leadership skills directly to their involvement in the Black Church. I did some research to identify the kinds of leadership lessons that Black churches might be sharing throughout history and currently. Through my research, I identified ten leadership lessons and corresponding leaders, whom I asked to let me know which lessons inspired them most. These rankings reveal the multifaceted nature of leadership skills cultivated within the Black Church, emphasizing not only spiritual and community-centric qualities but also essential attributes such as resilience, accountability, and effective communication. It's safe to say that not only is the Black Church the original social network for Black Americans, it has also served as the original business school.

It's important, now, to distinguish what defines the Black

Church, because not all churches with a Black leadership or even a congregation move within the Black Church cultural traditions. According to Dr. Henry Louis Gates Jr., in his book *The Black Church: This Is Our Story, This Is Our Song*, the distinction of the Black Church is primarily drawn along denominational lines, with those Black churches generally in the Baptist, Methodist, and Pentecostal traditions holding up the mantle of this cultural institution. These churches began in the South during slavery, all of them a result of Black people being segregated from white churches, and there was no separation of church and state. There were social and political meetings happening here. The Black Church became a nation within a nation, and the churches knew how to seize onto social cohesion and pool their finances to leverage economic empowerment. These churches formed large networks, across the nation. Many of these churches birthed Historically Black Colleges and Universities (HBCUs), and because these churches were primarily independent, across the South, they became targets for violence.

These churches, however, only represent a segment of the entire Black population's worship practices. Theirs are the sanctuaries where the worship centers liberation theology because they sprang from the suffering that required it. It should also be noted that Black people are and have been members of all sorts of churches, including Presbyterian, Catholic, Episcopalian, Church of Christ, and nondenominational among them, yet none of these churches position themselves as sites to counter white supremacy. These churches do not have the same histories as those designated as the core of the Black Church. Pew Research data also reveal that while some Black people claim to be Seventh Day Adventist, Jehovah's Witness, Mormon, and Muslim, 21 percent of Black respondents didn't claim any religion at all.

This is why the results of my survey are pretty striking: again, 82 percent of the high-performing Black leaders surveyed reported that they have attended Black churches extensively during their lifetime; 76 percent of respondents attributed their leadership skills directly to their involvement in the Black Church. Another 89 percent saw role models in the Black Church that influenced their leadership journey. Following are the top ten leadership skills these leaders identified as those they learned while attending the Black Church, ranked in order of percentage:

1. **Faith/Purpose:** A resounding **82 percent** of respondents attribute this as the most significant leadership skill learned in the Black Church, emphasizing the importance of spiritual grounding and purpose in leadership.
2. **Community organizing/involvement/volunteerism:** Second, with **66 percent**, underscoring the vital role of community engagement in Black leadership.
3. **Public speaking, presenting, or teaching:** This skill, valued by **56 percent**, highlights the ability to effectively communicate and inspire others.
4. **Resilience:** Demonstrated by **42 percent** of respondents, resilience is a critical quality for navigating challenges in leadership roles.
5. **Perseverance:** A notable **44 percent** recognize the importance of unwavering determination in leadership.
6. **Collaboration:** With **41 percent**, collaboration is recognized as a key skill, reflecting the emphasis on teamwork and unity within the Black Church.
7. **Accountability: 40 percent** acknowledge the significance of being accountable in leadership positions.

8. **Social justice/activism:** A substantial **32 percent** recognize the importance of advocating for justice and change within their leadership roles.
9. **Creativity/Innovation: 19 percent** acknowledge the value of thinking creatively and fostering innovation in leadership.
10. **Economic empowerment:** This skill is recognized by **18 percent**, reflecting the importance of economic stability and empowerment within the Black community.

The results reflect responses from 155 high-performing Black leaders, and they reveal a powerful testament to the enduring significance of Black churches in the lives of these leaders. The findings reveal that Black churches are not just places of worship but nurturing grounds for leadership development and community engagement. As I mentioned, the survey data also reveal 78 percent attended as children, highlighting the enduring tradition of passing down religious values and affiliations. This survey reaffirms the invaluable contribution of Black churches to leadership development and underscores their continued significance in shaping the future of Black leaders and communities.

Threats to This Leadership Wellspring

The COVID-19 pandemic prompted a shift to online services for many, showcasing the adaptability of these congregations in times of adversity, yet signaling that there could be an impending decline in the impact the Black Church may have on the leadership skills leaders glean from it, and ultimately those primed for leadership in corporate America. The active, in-person participation in church activities and ministry, combined with the diverse set of leadership skills acquired, is a hallmark of the holistic approach to leadership development within Black churches. The overwhelming presence of role models within these churches further solidifies their importance as sources of inspiration and guidance. Most significantly, respondents attributed a sizeable portion of their leadership skills to their involvement in the Black Church, highlighting the pivotal role these institutions play in shaping leaders. The survey also found a decline in these leaders' involving their children in the ministries of the Black Church, which could call into question the future of this crucial leadership development wellspring for the next generation of Black professionals.

According to Lifeway Research, a record number of all churches, Black or otherwise, shut their doors in 2019. The churches cited a severe challenge in attracting young people who had turned their backs on the institution and even their faith because their life choices didn't align with their church's political or social stances. Needless to say, the pandemic quarantine happened the next year and shuttered more church doors, and for those churches less affected, the challenge was influencing congregants to accept what had become the norm—online services, which many churches offered as an alternative to in-person services. The research goes on to say that Protestant pastors reported that typical church attendance is now only 85 percent of prepandemic levels. Another 2022 survey found that in spring 2022, 67 percent of Americans reported attending church at least once a year, compared with 75 percent before the pandemic. Did you catch that? Those people aren't even CMEs, those who attend on Christmas, Mother's Day, and Easter. Those numbers are according to the Survey Center on American Life and the University of Chicago.

Pew Research took it one step further, taking a look at church attendance in the Black community. The study found that most young people say they are "less religious" or attend religious services of any kind less than previous generations for reasons not unlike those the general population reported in the Lifeway study. Pew found that 49 percent of Black millennials and 46 percent of Black Gen-Zers reported that they "rarely" or "never" attend religious services. That tracks with what I learned from high-performing Black corporate leaders who responded to my brief survey on Black leaders and the Black Church. It bears repeating: A significant portion, 82 percent, have attended Black churches extensively during their lifetime, demonstrating the strong connection to these religious institutions within the community. Additionally, 78 percent attended as children, highlighting the enduring tradition of passing down religious values and affiliations. Could it be that the leadership pipeline is also influenced by this trend away from the church and in-person attendance? In response to my survey, fewer report attending in-person now, and many of them did not report placing the same emphasis on church attendance with their children.

Could leaders be missing out on a crucial aspect of the value of the traditional Black Church by skipping out on the experience or even limiting their experiences to a digital one? Could Black churches be diminishing their impact by ushering in more modern experiences that reflect mainstream evangelical churches that did not spring from the Black Church's uniquely American tradition of overcoming adversity? If Black women leaders are exiting the leadership pipeline in the middle of their careers, faster than any other group, and Black men have their own struggles to be seen and considered for leadership development opportunities, where else will Black leaders obtain a comprehensive and turnkey leadership lesson, especially if one-off leadership development experiences are only offered to those of so-called high potential or those precious few in the senior executive ranks?

Responding to the Call

For me, that photo of Dr. King flanked by a younger version of my home church pastor and the sisters of the church represents the lessons that emerge from the Black Church. Behind the glossy black, white, and gray facade of the photo, which seemed to freeze time, lies a story of courage, resilience, and faith—that of my pastor who took a chance, a risk, to be exact, by inviting the young civil rights leader to his pulpit to preach despite imminent danger. There were other leadership lessons from the pews, down the aisles, in the choir stand, and even in the Sunday School classrooms for Black leaders. Some of them were applied in the moment and inspired personal and professional development. The Black Church was by no means a spectator sport. To reap its full benefits, you were called off the bench, off the pew, at a very early age and thrust into the action. Certainly, the engine that drives any church is volunteerism, but this was a bit more. For example, I mentioned that a rite of passage for teenagers at my home church was to take on the teaching of an adult Sunday School class once a month when entering high school. While it wasn't as brutal as at the Apollo Theatre—where the Sandman could give you the big hook and tap dance on your figurative grave, if you didn't deliver—rightly dividing the word of truth to the satisfaction of the adults, many of them doctors, attorneys, politicians, and educators, you could very well get benched until an adult worked with you enough to bring you up to speed. It happened—often.

The adults were forgiving, however, gracious even. If you got stuck or forgot the words or notes, no doubt someone would yell out, "Take your time, baby!" But you only received so many of those until someone took you aside for more training.

Call and Response is a leadership book meant for leaders in business, but it centers Black leaders who recall the Black Church having a major impact on their lives and leadership skills. These leaders feel the institution moved them deeply and share how it continues to inform how they lead and succeed today, even in a predominately white corporate America. As I lay out the leadership lessons that these Black leaders say they learned, I will also lay out the evidenced-based case, with applied neuroscience and positive psychology for each one of the qualities, with data-driven insights. It is my goal to piece together the case that the Black Church and many of its traditions are a crucial resource in our society for preparing generation after generation of America's top Black business leadership, and that it has the power to inspire future generations of leaders if we allow it to.

However, the winds of change, societal trends, the modernization of worship services and church operations, and other issues challenge this. Are we willing to take intentional steps to salvage what could be leaks in the Black Church's own leadership pipeline to the highest levels of business? Can we address its own unique brain drain?

This isn't a book about Bible stories and the transformational power of those stories. While it is a bit nostalgic, evidence-based, and funny in places, this is my call, a challenge to preserve an unlikely cultural and informal leadership development resource that has and will continue to influence the future of businesses as we know it, if we respond swiftly, loudly, and deliberately.

1
FAITH AND PURPOSE
A Child Will Lead Them

If you listened closely, you could have heard the pitter-patter of little loafers and Mary Janes up and down the hallways of Sunday Schools across the United States on any given Sunday when I was growing up. It was no different in the Black Church. These tiny points of lights were learning their purpose in life and how to hold their heads up when faced with the negativity that the world had in store for them. This was especially important to Black children, born into the margins of society although they likely had no clue. There's very little research on the topic, but Black children tend to attend church more than their white counterparts. For those Black families who immigrate to the United States, church attendance is important for establishing connections and community that will fuel the life these families build. For sons and daughters of formerly enslaved people, church attendance is very much intertwined into their history in the United States. Thanks to migration patterns in search of life beyond Jim Crow, the Black Church tradition was carried from the South into the Northeast to major hubs like New

York, the Midwest to cities like Chicago and Detroit, and the West, where I and so many others have cousins, especially in Los Angeles and Oakland. In fact, I did my own research in 2015 for a campaign for AT&T that highlighted the impact the institution had on Black people as a whole. We called the Black Church "the original social network," according to the data we gathered for the "Inspired Mobility" campaign that featured Joseph "Rev Run" Simmons and others. But the Black Church wasn't simply a social network for adults. Children arguably made up just as much or more of Black Church attendees than anyone else, and the impact of the institution on them was and still is great. A study reported in the *Journal of Child and Family Studies* highlights that the impact the Black Church has on children is that it boosts their self-esteem and encourages them to thrive, and often in front of an audience.

Entrepreneur, board chair, and former four-time chief marketing officer for the Fortune 100 D. Keith Pigues says he really can't remember his first time in the Black Church because he said it felt like he was nearly born there. He credits most of what he knows today about leadership to the Black Church and by extension working in his father's tire retail and distribution business. His father was a man with an eighth-grade education, but proud of the learnings he gleaned from the Black Church. He passed it along to Keith in that business. For Keith, the Black Church wasn't simply about being tapped into a resourceful network. It was about what you learned there.

"So, we got a regular dose of development. We didn't think of it at that time from our experience in the church," Keith said. "Everything that I've learned fundamentally about people, about strategy, about serving, about connecting, about speaking, about teaching, about presenting, about communicating, writing, and about doing that in a way that creates value for other people . . . I learned either in the church or in my dad's businesses."

He's right. Looking back, it is clear that so much of what we saw as simply tradition and ritual was steeped in leadership development. It built our self-esteem. It prepared us for boardrooms.

"Everyone participated in vacation Bible school, at least everyone in our family did. And it was an opportunity to learn, to organize teams, to present," he said. "Everyone had to do some type of presentation for Easter. So, you had to learn the material, you had to practice, you had to speak—public speaking. And then we worked in all of those activities in and around adults who are in ministry and many times with the pastor or assistant pastor or associate pastors or ministry leaders."

Keith grew up in a family of modest means, but that didn't mean he didn't have high expectations for himself and his future. He says the lessons he learned from church and from his father—taught to him through his own informal education in church—prepared him in ways that he didn't fully realize until he was in business school at a prestigious university.

"When I got to graduate school, sitting in one of the MBA classes one day, it all came down on me like a ton of bricks," he said. "This strategy professor was explaining this term, and he was describing it and how you use it to develop business models and all of that. And I said to myself, 'My dad taught me that when I was about ten! So now you've given me a formal name, Mr. Business School professor, for something that you've had to get a PhD to teach!' My dad taught me that, and my dad grew up in a family of sharecroppers."

Learning "Your Why" Leads to Happiness

The most influential lesson Keith learned in the Black Church was one that the majority of high-performing Black leaders I surveyed strongly identified with: purpose. A resounding 82 percent of respondents attribute purpose, tied closely to their idea of faith, as the most significant leadership skill learned in the Black Church, emphasizing the importance of spiritual grounding and purpose in leadership. Personality psychologist Gordon Allport found that purposeful people have an assortment of better life outcomes, including being happier than people who do not know their purpose. Evidence from positive psychology shows that happy people are successful people. Allport's findings were reported in *Psychology Today* in June 2023: "Not only are people high in sense of purpose better at organizing their activities daily, but purposeful people are more likely to be happier. They also prioritize the people in their lives, which helps to promote better relationship outcomes."

It follows that people who learn their purpose have a higher emotional intelligence because of their ability to prioritize people. They also have a better handle on the importance of fostering relationships, which translates into formidable business acumen when it comes to building necessary rapport, relationships, and networks in business. Imagine obtaining all this, unknowingly, at a very young age, and at, of all places, the church.

Leaning into happiness also yields *more* success, a result of unrelenting focus. When I asked Keith to share what it is that he does now post-corporate life, in true form for a marketer, but also as a proud product of the church who actually has life coach written all over him, he promptly recited what he calls his "Life Purpose Statement."

"I help people get more out of work and life than they ever thought possible. That is my life purpose statement, and I do that," he said. "That is empowered or brought to life by speaking, writing, teaching, coaching, and advising."

It reads exactly like a well-polished value proposition, and rightfully so. Your life purpose is very much about your personal brand—the intentional experience you want others to have when they encounter you. Keith encountered Rick Warren's *The Purpose Driven Life* around the same time many of us did—at church in the early 2000s. It was likely the first time I saw the non–Black Church experience inspire Black churches everywhere. The core premise of Rick Warren's *The Purpose Driven Life* is that life's meaning is found through understanding and fulfilling God's purpose rather than pursuing personal ambitions or material success. The book is structured around five main purposes that Warren believes God has for every individual: worship, fellowship, discipleship, ministry, and mission. The book encourages readers to shift their focus from self-centered living to a God-centered life; it guides them to discover their purpose through faith, service, and community. This message was just what so many Black congregants were aching for. We needed and wanted to know our purpose, but insightfully, Keith drew a conclusion that I also came to long before I met Keith. These messages from pastors about purpose often leave congregants with the question "But how exactly?" and with no real action plan for finding out what zeroing in on and activating one's unique purpose actually entails, step by step. So after wrapping the Warren curriculum, Keith developed an entire program for the men in his church that addressed exactly that: how to actively discover your unique purpose and activate it in life, and it caught on with the women, couples, singles, and students.

Finding a Sense of Ownership and Responsibility

As a tween and teen, I discovered that it was the ritual of young people in my church to hang out in the halls between Sunday School and the 11:00 a.m. worship service, especially on days when we didn't have leadership responsibilities like junior usher board or choir. For some of us with doughnut glaze still on our lips or snacking on the hot pig in a blanket and juice we received in the fellowship hall, this was our time to form relationships . . . oh yes, and wait for Wallace to shoo us into church. It was inevitable. We really weren't supposed to call this deacon by his first name, and we didn't do it to his face, but it was definitely a sign of our collective annoyance at his disruption of our fellowship, which amounted to loitering. I still remember some of the boys breaking out into a sprint down the hall and whisper-yelling, "Wallace is coming!" Our cue to go hide in our respective restrooms. He couldn't come into the ladies' room, so the girls had a leg up.

I typically found my way into the sanctuary at that point. Sundays like this were few and far between. The students had responsibilities, but especially on the second Sunday of the month when the entire Sunday School and worship service were turned over to the youth. We did everything but preach. We took over the choir stand, the devotional period before worship (what turned into praise and worship later on), the responsive reading, or announcing the morning hymn. Musicians even turned the Hammond organ or piano over to a student if we had one talented enough. Eventually, we'd see the same thing with the drums. On some rare occasions, the adults extended an invitation to a storied, visiting teen or young adult preacher who would blow the roof off as if he were a seasoned preacher like the others who sat behind him. They waved huge white handkerchiefs at him, encouraging him to "PREACH!"

You've Just Been "Voluntold"

Accessibility catalyst and technology leader Heather Dowdy recalled that when she was twelve, an elder church leader pointed directly at her in the pew. "You," he said. "Come on up here." The word "no" never occurred to her, but she was definitely afraid of what she knew was next. He guided her by the hand onto the platform before hundreds of congregants at the Apostolic Faith Church in Chicago. She had been "voluntold" to lead the deaf ministry that day in American Sign Language (ASL). Until then, she had only really signed for her parents, because she had to. She was born to a deaf father and a mother who was hard of hearing. She was a CODA, a child of deaf adults. She began learning sign language at six months old, so she considered sign language to be her first language and the language with which she is most comfortable. However, she had no clue how ready for this big moment she actually was.

"He just pointed at me and said, 'You, come on. Get on up here. Interpret,'" she recalled. "I just knew he couldn't be talking about me because although the interpreters knew that I was a CODA and knew that I was fluent, this wasn't something we had talked about or practiced.

"And to go from being obscure, sitting in my seat, facing the stage, to being *on the stage* . . . I went up there, and I was nervous to have all these people looking like, 'Who is she?' . . . and to be so young! But I actually did a really good job, and even the interpreters were surprised at how well I did. And that just set off a pattern where they continuously asked me to come back. I think at that moment I realized that it was important for me to do it because I cared that there wouldn't be gaps in understanding the words."

It was indeed important that twelve-year-old Heather experienced this moment, because it set her on a path to bridge gaps between those with accessibility challenges and a world of rich experiences. Not only would she launch a career as an engineer to design and build the technology to do just that in some of the most behemoth and respected tech and entertainment companies, she would also serve presidents in a similar capacity. She served on the Biden administration's U.S. Access Board, appointed in 2022. This presidential appointment was no accident. Heather has more than fifteen years' experience developing and demonstrating accessible technology in mobile, web, and artificial intelligence. At the age of thirty-two, she initially turned down an opportunity to do sign interpretation for President Barack Obama at an event in Chicago in 2013. Self-doubt had set in, something she admits wouldn't have ever happened to her at twelve.

"The funny thing is being called up that day as a twelve-year-old, I didn't know to say no because an adult was asking me, but as a thirtysomething, I had learned some agency by then," she said. "So, I was like, 'No. No, thank you. I'm not going to do it. This isn't my day job.' And a couple of weeks before that, there was a fake interpreter in Florida during a press briefing with the mayor. And if you remember, there was a fake interpreter for Nelson Mandela's funeral. And so even though I knew the language and I could do this better than a lot of folks, I thought somebody's going to find out that this is not what I do for my day job and try to cancel me, and I don't need all of that. No, thank you."

Something shifted for her, however, and she remembered that sign interpretation was her calling and a gift from God, and once more He used someone else to force the issue. She was "voluntold" yet again.

"Somebody I knew who was organizing the event was like, 'I'm putting your name down anyway.'" At that moment, Heather realized, "When God calls you, it's because He already knows you're ready."

To this day she wishes she had a photo of herself at twelve years old signing at the Apostolic Faith Church at Thirty-Eighth and Indiana on the south side of Chicago so that she could place it side by side with the newspaper photo of her signing for President Obama. She said it would be a reminder of her purpose, following through on a crucial leadership lesson from the Black Church to show empathy for a group of people who were in these spaces and wanted access to what everyone else was receiving even if they weren't fully integrated into the congregation or audience. That she was there to be that critical bridge, to not only interpret, but to teach. Heather says she discovered her spiritual gift of teaching in the Black Church. Sign language was her form of speaking and presenting.

Sparking Empathy and Purpose in the Smallest of These

Heather and Keith have very different stories, but both ring out truths about sparking the value of purpose and empathy to create awesome leaders even in children. Keith empathized with congregants wanting to uncover their own unique purpose in life. Heather empathized with members of the deaf ministry in her church, wanting to connect with the powerful words and songs in Sunday service and ultimately feel as if they belonged in that congregation.

Our brains are equipped to empathize. In fact, according to research from the Department of Neuroscience at the Icahn School of Medicine at Mount Sinai, our brains fire off when empathy, the perception of others' emotions, is ignited within us. Most specifically, it is that center in the brain that engages so that we feel empathy for pain, not only emotional but also physical. That area of the brain is called the anterior insular cortex. A child who can tap into empathy, such a highly nuanced emotion, to begin to relate to what someone else must be feeling is already beginning to train their brain to do what some adults struggle to do. That could be because the anterior insular cortex is only where the empathetic activity occurs, which implies that there is something that should trigger it. Experts say that empathy is actually a skill, and although children as young as three begin to sense the emotions of others and how the impact of actions they take can affect others, empathy is ultimately a learned behavior that takes practice. In the case of these two leaders, Heather and Keith, empathy was an amazing intrinsic motivator that not only drove them to their purpose but also pushed them to do more at a young age, build on that through young adulthood, and then sustain it through a lifetime of work.

In fact, empathy seems to be a key to purpose. It's difficult to separate the two. If these Black leaders are learning empathy and purpose at a young age, chances are they will have a special impact as adult leaders in business and the community.

The World Health Organization (WHO) recently listed these specific challenges in workplaces for employees:

- excessive workloads;
- long, isolated, or inflexible work hours;

- psychologically unsafe work environments;
- poor work-life integration and limited to nonexistent support from leaders.

The global nonprofit Catalyst recently pointed out the importance and impact of empathetic leadership on issues like these in a recent study of 899 employees, because it

- leads to innovation,
- boosts employee engagement,
- positively influences the work-life of employees,
- fosters inclusivity.

According to the National Library of Medicine, the relationship between *empathic concern* and the tendency to experience positive emotion has received much less empirical attention, though the results from two studies, one by Robinson, Emde, and Corley in 2001 on dispositional cheerfulness, and the other by Rothbart, Ahadi, and Hershey in 1994 on temperament and social behaviors in children, suggest that there is a positive relationship between *empathic concern* and the tendency to experience positive emotion. Note that both these studies focus on how much of this behavior is adopted in childhood.

According to a 2020 article by Daniel Goleman from Korn Ferry titled "How Purpose and Emotional Intelligence Connect," "This sense of how we might help other people very often leads to the conviction that we have a purpose greater than just helping ourselves—and this compels us to take action on their behalf." The author goes on to write that having soft skills like emotional intelligence and the empathy it yields is the only way a purpose-driven company can succeed. Empathy and purpose may naturally tie into the Black Church's commitment to service through its ministries, and those ministries have embedded in them big concepts in doing business.

Little Ministries Meant Big Lessons in Service and Business

For as long as Keith, the four-time chief marketing officer, could remember, every aspect of his life was focused on the church because his parents and grandparents, aunts and uncles received most of their formal training and their faith there and not in educational institutions. He said he loved every minute of being in church and working in ministry. His first recollection of serving in ministry and leading was when he decided to join the junior usher board. In Black churches, there was typically a kids-meal version of the main course, no matter what it was:

For every mass choir, there was a junior choir.

For each worship service or training union there was a children's or youth church or component.

So of course, the usher board had a youth usher ministry.

This was the leadership pipeline at church, but none of us knew to call it that.

"The first time I can remember is when I was a member of the Ushers Ministry. That was my thing. So, everyone, by the way, at that time, had to pick a ministry. You didn't have an option," Keith said. "I became a leader with the Youth Ushers. I remember having to help people with training. We'd get new people, and you'd have to train them on what their job is. We'd have meetings. We were learning a little bit of Robert's Rules of Order informally. You were required to keep up with people to make sure they showed up."

All of this happened while learning good customer service, recognition, team morale, and helping the congregants and church leaders with hospitality. Everyone, once you became a member, was expected to serve and do so with excellence, "as unto the Lord."

"We had events and outings where we had fun and we would recognize people for their contribution," Keith said. "We would have to hold people accountable when they didn't do what they said they were going to do. And you had to make sure that every Sunday or every event, everybody was dressed in uniform, your shoes were shined to a tee, the ties were on, the knots were tied correctly, and the tie was the right length, that the shirt was bright white, that you had the black pants on and you had a nice belt on."

While Keith didn't know at the time that he was learning important business and leadership skills as a member of the junior ushers, looking back, he cherishes them.

THE LEADERSHIP LESSONS

Recognize that your purpose has always been present. Remember that you are *uncovering* or *activating* what has been there all along. Your life experiences have prepared you.

Stop waiting until you feel 100% ready. If someone pushes you out front, consider the opportunity before brushing it off. They likely see something in you that you haven't yet. Purpose doesn't require perfection—it requires movement. Many high achievers second-guess themselves, even when they are more than qualified.

Define your life purpose in a clear statement. Clarity brings focus. Take time to write a one-sentence statement that defines the impact you want to have on the world. This will shape your decisions, leadership, personal brand, and most importantly, your happiness.

Engage empathy as the gateway to purpose. Research shows that empathy is tied to emotional intelligence and business success. Originating in the anterior insular cortex, empathy can be built as a skill. Identify a need in others, then set out on a path to insert your talents.

Activate purpose through service. Purpose isn't a one-time revelation; it's a practice. It is activated through consistent action. Volunteer. Teach. Coach. Mentor. Look for opportunities to serve where your strengths align.

COACHING QUESTIONS

Where did you first uncover your sense of purpose, and how can you engage it to lead others in business as you aspire for the next level?

What can you learn from the childhood experiences of these leaders in the Black Church, and how can you apply it to your own leadership quest in your life today?

CALL AND RESPONSE

How can you build your empathetic leader muscle in the work that you do today for better impact?

If you are struggling with a sense of purpose, take some time to outline the things that you value and let that guide you. List at least three big concepts or ideas that drive or motivate you.

Recount a transformative story from your childhood, whether in the Black Church or not, that shapes who you are as a leader today.

2
COMMUNITY
The Covenant and Circle Unbroken

The idea of community and connection has increasingly fascinated me over the years. Especially since delving into the science of it. Until recently, thinking of the word *community* conjured a place, a neighborhood perhaps, maybe even a suburb. The word can even refer to a group of people, not simply a physical place. We've also heard the term *the Black Community*, a group of people who may share skin color as well as a cultural bond across the diaspora. As such, community can be fostered within organizations like the church, a sorority or fraternity, even schools, workplaces, and nonprofits. We see organizations like media outlets attempting to create community with the development of events, programming, and networking opportunities, on- and offline, that reach beyond their pages and streams or broadcasts. Some may require payment or a membership to receive access, like the advisory panels we see at some big national business publications. All of these entities understand the power of gathering people, whether virtually or in person, around similar values, rituals, beliefs, and, more practically, the output that emerges from those circles of people. It creates a bond and, from a marketing perspective, more loyalty to their brands because you've created an experience that involves the people.

Neuroscience research reveals that connection and community both cause our brains to secrete a hormone called oxytocin. It's popularly known as "the love hormone" and sometimes "the trust hormone," which causes human beings to bond. Considering that the opposite of community is isolation, there is the potential for its strength in providing connection and even some security, especially for those seeking someplace to belong. Neuroscience also points to love as being the strongest of the ten positive emotions, which include joy, serenity, awe, amusement, inspiration, gratitude, interest, pride, and hope. Positive psychology points to positive emotion as something that moves humans forward faster in their personal and professional development because emotions are triggered by one's values.

Those that believe in biblical scripture abide by the principle that God is love, as the book of I John says. Therefore, it follows that the community and connections fostered by the Black Church can be a powerful phenomenon because that sense of belonging sits at the intersection of two powerful cultural paradigms: religion and race. The Church becomes a place where we can all generally agree, where Blackness is unquestionably centered, and where worship is grounded in the liberation of a people who have historically fought for their lives—in the time of slavery and during the 1950s and '60s for their civil and human rights. Today the Black Church continues to fight to hold on to those rights politically; the fight ensures being seen, heard, and in many spaces, especially the workplace, respected. At its core, this is what differentiates the Black Church from predominantly white churches. Black people historically have *needed* their church for everything in life: social connections and community, access to services and resources, freedom to express themselves about the woes of the reality outside of the church doors, and community organizing. Yet what I consider to be the greatest societal accomplishment of the Black Church—besides producing good citizens, leaders, and service in the communities where they live—is the Civil Rights Movement. It took community, strong connections, and determination to make it happen.

The Black Church meant progress for Black people because it fostered upward mobility. Where else could you sit beside Black elected officials, Black teachers, Black doctors, Black attorneys, Black entertainers, Black bus drivers, Black nurses, and Black housekeepers all in the same pew? All of them were gathered around the content that inspired them, the rhythms and triads they loved and that uplifted them, and the preaching they could relate to—with a fiery delivery and a nice dose of social justice woven into the message.

It is no wonder that Martin Luther King Jr. lamented on *Meet the Press* in 1960: "I think it is one of the tragedies of our nation . . . that eleven o'clock on Sunday morning is one of the most segregated hours, if not the most segregated hours, in Christian America." But there is a sustaining reason for it. According to an *Axios* report on race and the state of the American church, "Some well-known white churches and denominations were tied to efforts to justify and maintain slavery, while Black churches formed in response to segregation." And while nearly 60 percent of megachurches reported being multiracial, the Black culture in those churches is typically watered down or tempered to appeal to broader worship tastes and styles. Sometimes, it is nonexistent. Some of the more contemporary churches have done away with the gospel choirs, an art form birthed from within the National Baptist Convention and that is a uniquely Black art form, in favor of praise teams and bands that play contemporary Christian music—many of them paid professionals. Still, more multicultural churches make no mention of social justice issues. Other newer churches have online campuses for "virtual church" that do not require members to join the congregation in person, and while they may host small groups online throughout the week, the opportunity for real community is lost. I call this the modernization of the Black Church, because as it grows to memberships in the thousands, many of the traditions go by the wayside. And while church consultants may argue that tradition is one of the primary causes for younger generations' disinterest in attending, it is also becoming apparent that this is one of the reasons why some Black children and young people are beginning to miss out on the unique leadership development opportunities that the Black Church historically offered. How can you sing in the kids' choir if you aren't present in person, or if you have to audition to sing onstage with the praise team? That can be intimidating.

Where Sarah Became Madam Walker

One of my favorite historical figures gained her footing in the Black Church. While most know her for her accomplishment as the first woman of any race to become a self-made millionaire businesswoman in the United States, little is shared about how the AME church poured into Madam C. J. Walker and essentially provided her with the foundation required to build her business empire. The Black Church provided the community and resources she needed to build her network and learn about leadership all while attending church and benefiting from outreach programs. Her great-great-granddaughter, biographer, and keeper of her legacy, former journalist, author, and producer A'Lelia Bundles, shared more.

"Madam Walker was very involved with the AME church," Bundles said. "The women of St. Paul AME in St. Louis were her most important mentors when she still was a washerwoman."

Sarah Breedlove McWilliams, who would later go by the more famous name Madam Walker, was only twenty-one years old and a widowed single mother when the members of St. Paul AME took her and her daughter, Lelia, in at their lowest point. Sarah arrived as a part of a migration of Black Americans trying to find their way to Kansas City, where they'd heard there was farmland for the taking. Sarah and her daughter stopped short of Kansas City, along with 1,600 others who were weary from the journey, and instead stayed in St. Louis because her brother had moved there some years before. He had established himself in the St. Louis community through his membership at St. Paul, the oldest Black Protestant church in St. Louis and the oldest of any Black Protestant church west of the Mississippi River. There, beyond Bible study, the women's ministries ensured that Sarah regained her footing by providing a safe haven to rebuild her life from the inside out by offering food, clothing, housing, and life-skills and educational classes. The women were so well-networked within the community that they were able to offer free childcare at the local orphanage so that her daughter, considered a "half-orphan," could stay there while Sarah worked during the week. It turned out that St. Paul church members had key roles at the facility, so those arrangements were easily made. She learned leadership skills from the ladies who ran the ministries and clubs, watching them move with grace, dignity, and determination, navigating the community through connections. They were mission driven, and Sarah was a direct recipient of their impact. This left a deep impression on Sarah, who eventually became active in the very clubs and ministries that supported her through tough times. Before long, she was able to use her skills to lead efforts under these women because she knew the programs so well.

A'Lelia Bundles contributed an article to an edition of the *AME Church Review* published in 2000 that detailed this crucial time in the life of Madam Walker. She wrote: "In addition to the friendships that Sarah gained, through the networks at St. Paul, she was exposed to important lessons about racial pride, institution building, and economic development." This church was proud to say that it was the only church in St. Louis built "by and for Negroes," and it had a long history of activism and social justice. Built in the early 1800s, the church held clandestine reading classes for enslaved people, a daring act as it was illegal to teach enslaved people living in "slave states" to read. It's important to note that this activity predates even the founding of Historically Black Colleges and Universities (HBCUs) in 1837. The nine-hundred-member church was said to have had beautiful stained-glass windows and one of the most magnificent pipe organs in the city. The church members were active in other more public and political efforts, such as bussing hundreds of Black citizens into St. Louis from other parts of the country to protest lynchings through fasting and prayer. Bishops and other clergy who visited spoke to the people of St. Paul AME about everything from global issues concerning mission work to local social and racial issues that directly affected their membership.

Sarah took all of this in and built a network of her own. She dreamed of having her own business, one that would solve an age-old problem for Black women who struggled to care for their hair so that it would be healthy and also look attractive. Having issues with her own hair, she was inspired to develop her own product. Eventually, Sarah got on her feet, and with her new venture, connections, and vision, she moved to Denver, Colorado, where she joined the Shorter Community AME Church where her widowed sister-in-law was already a member. She was instantly "plugged in" and began to establish her hair-care business while becoming an active member of the church. She took the leadership lessons she'd observed and learned at St. Paul and multiplied them, growing her influence, impact, and eventually her sales force of women entrepreneurs; the Black Church was her home base and leadership launchpad. Eventually she married a man named Charles Johnson Walker and became known as Madam C. J. Walker, establishing her company after the same name. The rest is history. Madam Walker would move a few more times before her death in May 1919, and each time, she connected with the prominent AME church in that city, at least four in total, building relationships with the bishops and the women who made the wheels of each of those churches turn. Each time she grew her reach as a philanthropist, businesswoman, and good citizen.

Community and Connection Are the Jet Fuel for Happiness and Success

Besides being an example of women helping and empowering other women, Madam Walker's story of a broke washerwoman turned thriving millionaire businesswoman is an example of the massive impact the Black Church had on a singular human being and her trajectory as a leader. It speaks to the power of community and the connections it fosters. Sounds simple enough, but when you consider the science behind it, you'll begin to understand the incredible power to reverse the destruction that isolation can bring. Imagine what might have happened to Sarah had St. Paul AME Church not taken her in.

Connection and community have a profound impact on well-being and success for leaders. Specifically, connection and community do three things:

Alleviate stress and promote well-being. Research from the University of California, Berkeley, shows that this reduction of stress and anxiety enhances mental health and cognitive function.

Enhance resilience in adversity. Studies by the American Psychological Association reveal that strong social networks help individuals cope with challenges and bounce back from setbacks.

Help develop a sense of belonging, self-esteem, and fulfillment. Research from the *Journal of Personality and Social Psychology* highlights that a sense of belonging positively inspires self-esteem and overall life satisfaction.

Positive psychology emphasizes throughout its most popular research that community and connectedness are triggers for positive emotion, and you can infer through Madam Walker's story with St. Paul AME that she could feel this sense of love, hope, and pride while receiving the support from its parishioners. When you don't have the worries of survival at the forefront of your mind, you are free to dream again, focus on those dreams, and ultimately pursue them relentlessly. This is what the Black Church has done for numerous business leaders of today, although many of them didn't have to come from rock bottom to reap the benefits. It did provide them with an empowering space that fueled joy and happiness in challenging moments, whether from society or from work, to free their minds enough to dream.

"What I liked most about it was just the family, the community," Fortune 500 business consultant D. Keith Pigues said. "I mean, you just felt safe. It's like when you were there with the other people in the church, you were just safe. It's a place where we came together, and we were just us. I just enjoyed it."

Belonging is something that Black leaders yearn for in the workplace and society. Knowing that a historic and cultural institution has been an originator of belonging for Black people since its beginnings makes it feel like a safe place for many, a place to learn, thrive, and grow.

The Circle Unbroken Is Covenant and Power

About 66 percent of those high-performing Black leaders who responded to my survey said that they learned about community, organizing, involvement, and volunteerism in the Black Church, whether through their involvement in ministries and outreach or by watching it modeled. Community building for many Black corporate leaders is second nature, something they rarely consciously think about because it comes naturally for them. Some say that it's because they saw it so often and at a young age within their churches. Fostering community within the Black Church and outside of it, reaching and resonating with its ministries and efforts concentrically throughout neighborhoods, cities, towns, suburbs, and sometimes even the nation, meant more than simply joining a Bible study or a small group, or even engaging in acts of service outside of the church. It also meant witnessing firsthand from a young age that community as it unfolded in the Black Church implied organization, politics, a chain of command, and ultimately power, as CEO Xavier Williams shared.

"I saw how the pecking order and political capital works in the church. So, if you think about the pastor, the deacon board, the deaconess board, the ministerial staff, you think about all the different machinations ... when you're talking about community, there was a structure in place where there was a power base."

Williams noticed from a young age that those individuals were driving the sense of community and influenced how things were done and who did the things. Whether it was that one person who was in this position because they were linked to the pastor or because they were in a certain fraternity or sorority, or they went to a certain school or belonged to a social or professional organization, the web of relationships and how that affected the community was something to behold. Other leaders shared that whether it was from a long-standing relationship between a grandparent and the pastor, or was from a mother who happened to be on the board of an organization of another member's nonprofit organization, the power that people wielded came directly from their connections to other people; these connections formed the community and gave individuals and the communities a palpable power.

It's amazing to reflect that what scholars have termed "community power" is at the center of Black America's oldest cultural institution, and it is the same dynamic that is prevalent in corporate America. Social capital, relational equity, and the politics of connections dictate influence, relevance, status, and stature, and ultimately the power to get things done. Scholars at the University of Wisconsin–Stevens Point described community power this way in a 2005 white paper on the topic: "Power in a community is the ability to affect the decision-making process and the use of resources, both public and private, within a community or watershed group. Power is simply the capacity to bring about change. It is the energy that gets things done."

Proximity to this community power had a positive impact on the self-esteem of these leaders. I definitely felt the impact. Simply walking through the doors at Good Street Baptist Church, I knew that I would, in the course of attending one worship service on any given Sunday, come into contact with plenty of my mother's sorority sisters who were members of the largest graduate chapter in Dallas. I'm a member there today—the Alpha Xi Omega chapter of Alpha Kappa Alpha Sorority, Inc., which celebrated its hundredth anniversary in 2025. All these ladies were either well-known and respected educators, elected officials, professionals, community organizers, or the influential wives of doctors, attorneys, judges, other elected officials, and pastors. My father's Kappa Alpha Psi connections weren't lost on me either. A well-placed letter of reference from my father helped one of my church friends into the local graduate chapter when he was ready to seek membership.

Still, sometimes, the Black Church community will find you where you work and live, right when you need it most, and it isn't fancy with ties to any sororities or fraternities. That happened to Michael C. Hyter when he was just beginning his career. He's currently the president and CEO of the Executive Leadership Council, an organization that describes itself as "the preeminent membership organization for Black CEOs, board directors, and the most senior Black executives at Fortune 1000, Global 500 and equivalent companies." Mike previously worked as chief diversity officer for global recruitment and consulting firm Korn Ferry. With his mission to bring more Black leaders through the pipeline into the E- and C-Suites and boards of corporate America, Mike recalls a time when the hands and feet of the Black Church cradled him in community and provided unlikely sponsorship, pulling him through that very pipeline, and from a very unlikely place.

Just out of college and in his first year as a personnel management trainee at a large department store in the heart of Detroit, Mike faced his first experience with overt racism in the workplace. Disheartened at what he saw, he was at a crossroads, wondering if he had made the right decision to turn down other lucrative roles in human resources (HR) or as a salesperson at a larger company. He also found himself on the elevator with an elevator operator named Mrs. Bell.

"She said, 'What's wrong, baby?' And I just leveled with her. I said, you know, I don't know if I'm in a good space because I took on this job and I'm working with people that don't like us. And I really feel like this isn't the right spot for me. And I'm just sort of sad about it. So, thank you for asking," he said. "And she asked me if I was open to meeting her and a few other people in the second basement of the store the following morning. And because I was an assistant HR person and it was a group of employees, I didn't know whether there was a complaint, if it was a union thing, or something. So, I agreed to do it because in my role, I wanted to be available to employees who wanted a private meeting with me. And so I went, I met them there."

Mike couldn't have anticipated what happened next. It turned out that this meeting in the second basement was a bit of a routine prayer and planning meeting among elevator operators, janitors, and service technicians at the department store, a secret meeting, and an underground railroad.

He went on to share what the elevator operator, who he described was like a grandmother, did next: "Mrs. Bell announced to the group, 'Mr. Hyter is going through a rough time with the management of this store. And we all, you all know, and you met, and you spent time with this young man,' and everybody nodded. And she says, 'And you know, we love this young man because he's representative of the best of us. He's from Michigan State. I want to declare in front of all these people that he's going to be successful. We're not gonna let him fail.'"

Then Mrs. Bell, who he recalled in the moment was the first lady at an area church, asked everyone in attendance to gather around him. They laid hands on him and prayed. But it didn't stop there. These service professionals made it their mission to inform Mike about every little thing that happened in that nineteen-floor, 2.2-million-square-foot facility. They became his eyes and ears, and with that inside information, he was able to turn the tide on his work experience there at the department store, and within a few years got promoted to HR manager and eventually vice president.

"So, all of a sudden, I became this uber-successful, first-time-in-history HR person that was in touch with what the employees were doing or in touch with where there were problems. And my success overshadowed the hatred with these two old guys who were basically just calling it in," he said. These service workers, who were classically invisible, had formed their own community, pulled together by their faith under the leadership of a woman clearly influenced by her church. They leveraged the power of their community to lift up a young professional to heights none of them had yet seen. This intergenerational connection is something that is core to the Black Church experience. Mike recognized a "church mother" in that moment, and it hadn't occurred to him before, but did he ever feel the impact?

He said that the experience shaped his leadership philosophy, inspiring him to become a "Mrs. Bell" for others by actively supporting and mentoring people in his network.

Rev. Cokiesha Bailey Robinson, associate dean of mentoring and cross cultural engagement at Grace College (a Bible college in rural Indiana), an author, and an ordained minister, says there is power in the intergenerational friendships that can be found in the Black Church and its multigenerational community. Her father, Dr. E. K. Bailey, founded the Concord Church in Dallas; I've attended the church for more than twenty years. My father worked in the stewardship ministry with Cokiesha Bailey Robinson's father when I was a toddler. He passed away in 2003, but my parents still consider his wife, Dr. Sheila Bailey, to be a friend. It's how I know Rev. Robinson. I call her my "Reverend Doctor Sisterfriend." We are only a few years apart and consider each other extended family, the kind of family you make at church because it's even more meaningful than friendship, even if you don't talk every day.

According to Rev. Robinson, "The friendships have been multigenerational. Some of my parents' friends from Bishop College stayed their friends, even when they became their pastor and first lady. Now my siblings and I are friends with their kids. And now I've been called so many places away from Dallas, but those Concord and Dallas relationships remain. And I'm fortified because leadership lessons were also tied to eternal multigenerational friendships."

CALL AND RESPONSE

Knowing Who You Are and Who You Know Strengthens the Connections That Make Things Happen

Many of my friends were elders in my church. The adult Sunday School class that I taught once a month as a teen was led by the head of the local masons, a "grand poohbah," we would joke to each other within the youth group. He had a velvet, tasseled hat and golden medallions to prove it, but he cared. I remember the day he learned that I was accepted into TCU. He had applied back when it was segregated, and they sent him packing to Jarvis College, the HBCU they ran in Marshall, Texas. The tears of joy I saw in his eyes! He wanted to see me fly and was always willing to help or put in a good word.

"It was always taught to me in church that it wasn't about me, it was about the person behind me and who are you pulling up, you know, pulling up to your side and pushing ahead of you," said Xavier Williams, wireless company CEO and retired Fortune 10 senior executive. "That was definitely a lesson that was consciously and subconsciously imparted on me because, and I just can't tell you how many things that I do now are just subconscious because of the way I grew up and especially during my time in church."

You could witness the power of community in the hallways as the older deacons or elders stopped young men to simply pour out words of wisdom. Even the notables in our church were role models who showed us their humility by being a part of the local body and serving for a greater purpose that was larger than themselves. There was a well-known senator in the mix at Good Street; he was one of the more prominent deacons. He was also an attorney, and for a while was esteemed as our local Johnnie Cochran—from O.

J. Simpson's so-called Dream Team. As things would have it, that prominent deacon knew Mr. Cochran, which is why I met Cochran at the age of twenty-two. I emceed the church scholarship banquet with a local anchor who happened to be my mentor. Mr. Cochran was our keynote speaker for the evening. He had just wrapped the "Trial of the Century," which catapulted him to near rock stardom in the Black community. Mr. Cochran's attendance was about the love and respect that he had for Pastor Clark and giving back. His presence would draw more attention and attendance to this scholarship banquet, which would help fund graduating seniors' next steps toward higher education. He was giving back and quietly leading by example and helping others along.

A member of the Texas House of Representatives was also a member of our church. He was one of the more popular Sunday School teachers and had lectured at my parent's alma mater at some point. Church members seemed to treat him with some of the same respect they offered our pastor. He was long-winded, so I usually excused or distracted myself the minute I saw him step up to the podium, but my brother-in-law's brother worked for him for years in Austin, and his mother adored him, so I needed to watch how I spoke of this deacon around my in-laws. These larger-than-life people didn't seem unapproachable or inaccessible to me at the time, nothing out of the ordinary. But I did admire the fact that he was giving back, a mentor to many who had their sights set on a career in politics or at the university.

There was a prominent judge in our congregation. My father really admired him, and when I went to work for the TV station and covered the courts, I knew I was welcome in his courtroom. If I notified his wife ahead of time, she would make sure that he knew I was headed downtown.

Then, there was this annual occurrence that I used to take for granted until one year all the news cameras showed up and we actually allowed them into the sanctuary. Historical figures weren't new to our church, not even celebrities, but this individual was larger than life and would become even larger as he brought the national civil rights and political scene directly into our pulpit. My father ran the sound system and tape ministry; well, even that had its perks. Often, my sister and I were responsible for getting the lapel mic downstairs to the pastor or guest preacher before they walked into the sanctuary. We were like Pastor Clark's grandkids; at least that's how it felt to me. So, as you entered his office and the guest minister was there, Pastor Clark would introduce you to the guest minister as the person who would supply the microphone: "Brother Smith's daughter . . . Michelle." It's one thing when you were miking up the pastor of the church from a few miles away or even from another state. It's quite another when it is Rev. Jesse Jackson. Once a year, Rev. Jackson made his way to Good Street to preach, but one year, in 1984, he announced that he was running for president of the United States, and he brought the national spotlight with him to the pulpit to preach.

Our community at Good Street was strong because of connections like these, and it wasn't until I was older that I realized that I had witnessed firsthand these leaders in action. I had observed these leaders many times before I had even graduated high school.

My church wasn't the only one like this. When you consider that very few Black people attended church with white people even into the 1960s and '70s, if you were Black and attended church, the local and national Black notables who attended church had to go somewhere, and it was likely at a sanctuary near you. Leadership literally dripped from the pews, podiums, and pulpits in the Black Church, yielding a powerfully networked community, somewhat aware of its prowess, but not fully. My home church was a shining example of this. Imagine meeting the second Black person ever in history to mount a national campaign for the White House, or watching my pastor call out country singer Charley Pride to come sing a verse or two of a hymn impromptu, or sitting a few rows behind "Who's Making Love" R&B, soul, and blues singer Johnnie Taylor when the pastor also called him to the choir stand to sing a few lines of "Amazing Grace." I can still see his press and curl in my mind's eye . . . or it might have been a relaxer. I'm not certain.

Both Pride and Taylor were leaders in their industry; they projected resilience and excellence. Pride was a former Negro League baseball player and, according to many sources, was the first major Black superstar in country music. Taylor was thrice Grammy nominated and inducted into a few notable halls of fame, including R&B and Blues. Watching these weighty celebrities be "voluntold" to perform on the spot also leveled the playing field a bit, knowing that even they weren't exempt from the traditions in the Black Church, and this riffing without much preparation is something many of us learned to do and then took with us into the corporate realm. As we were told, "If you are ready, you don't have to get ready, so always be ready."

For many of us, though, the power of the community wasn't found in the celebrities we knew or in the shared peppermint between A-and-B selections from the choir. We found that power in connections with other church members who would take care of you in happy and sad times, forming unbreakable bonds, producing unspeakable joy. Like the grandmother of my high school sweetheart who stayed with me after surgery when my mother and father had to work; her grandson and I had broken up years before, but that was insignificant. She had become my grandmother too. Or it might have been the trustee member who opened her lovely home to host bridal and baby showers for young blushing brides or expectant mothers. My sister met and married her husband at our church. Like others, families joined in holy matrimony and made the Black Church one big family, and even more of a political beast to navigate. You had to be careful what you said around everyone, because you could never be quite sure who was related to whom.

"Our pastor, when I was growing up, was one of my grandmother's best friends. They grew up together, so we had a very close relationship with him and his wife and kids," Fortune 500 business consultant D. Keith Pigues said. "My grandmother was head of the mothers' board when she was older. Our family was so connected to the ministry leaders that it was just like an extension of family for us. So, it was home. It was home in so many ways."

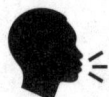

THE LEADERSHIP LESSONS

Build relationships—you are only as strong as your network. Community is more than just connection; it is a strategic asset that can shape your career. Identify your "power base"—the decision-makers, influencers, and key stakeholders in your organization or industry. Build relationships that create mutual value, not just access.

Learn from every level and generation—mentorship works both ways. Strong leaders do not just seek guidance from those ahead—they also learn from those behind them. Build a three-way mentorship network—someone ahead of you, a peer at your level, and an emerging leader who can offer fresh insights.

Provide the support your team needs so they can thrive—foster psychological safety. Great leaders create environments where people feel valued, supported, and empowered. Be an active sponsor for someone in your network. Go beyond mentorship—advocate for them, open doors, and champion their growth.

Leverage community power to drive change. The best leaders do not act alone—they mobilize others. Successful leaders know how to rally people around a mission. Identify a cause, policy, or initiative in your organization that needs momentum. Mobilize your network to influence decisions and make a measurable impact.

Invest in community—isolation is the enemy of happiness and growth. Research confirms that strong networks reduce stress, increase resilience, and foster long-term success. Make relationship building a core leadership skill. Engage in industry communities, peer networks, and mentorship groups that support both your success and well-being.

COACHING QUESTIONS

What can you do starting today to intentionally create connections inside of work and outside of work to create powerful, purposeful relationships?

What can the community-building traditions in the Black Church teach us about navigating the hierarchies within corporate and other business entities?

At what points do you feel most isolated in the workplace, and what best practices from the Black Church can you engage to begin to build connections?

What communities do you tap into when you need a boost of happiness to get you through a challenging time at work? How can you foster deeper connections?

3
SPEAKING

The Power of Storytelling and Performance

Recently, my daughter and I went to the movie theater at the big mall about thirty miles away from our home. We typically finish the movie and then wander around the acres of retail inside the mall. One of our favorite shops is the Lego Store. It's attached to Lego's mini theme park, Legoland. My daughter wanted a new building set, so we dipped inside. As we meandered through the aisles, my eye caught something. It was a set from Lego's botanicals line—yellow jonquils. I got so excited, but my eleven-year-old was confused.

"Why are you so excited about that?" she said, like a typical uninterested tween.

"Well, I know you may not understand, but I have never seen this word written before," I responded. "It's something my first pastor used to say as a metaphor when he was *really* preaching. He spoke of the stars dancing through the sky like 'debutantes at a coming-out party,' and while the next line escapes me, he indeed referred to yellow jonquils as a part of that picture he so eloquently painted. I have to snap a picture and send it to your grandparents!"

Jonquil is another word for *daffodil*. It was fascinating to hear Dr. C. A. W. Clark refer to these flowers from the pulpit. He had attended school through the seventh grade; he then taught himself so comprehensively he was accepted into Bishop College, a now-closed historically Black college attended by many Black preachers. Clark's reference to jonquils was one of my earliest memories of his storytelling. He always painted a picture in his sermons. Some say that he sounded just like C. L. Franklin. If you heard Clark, and I did often because my dad ran the sound and tape ministry for years, you might say so as well. I choose to believe that C. L. Franklin sounded like Pastor Clark because he didn't have a huge platform in the form of a record label and the Queen of Soul as his daughter. However, according to historians, he had more than twenty long-playing records of his sermons, most of them on Franklin's label. It's common knowledge that many preachers attempted to sound like the man who was known in Black preaching circles as "The Preacher's Preacher" and "Little Caesar" because of his small stature. *Ebony* magazine frequently listed Clark as one of the fifteen greatest preachers in America because of his amazing oratorical abilities, and some say that he perfected the art of "whooping." I know this because toward the end of his career at the Good Street Baptist Church, a *Dallas Morning News* reporter who had taken on a personal project to track down the origins of the art of whooping was told by many preachers and pastors across the country that she needed to visit the church at 3110 Bonnie View Road to witness this great wonder. She reached out to me to make it happen. Not to be confused with tuning, where the preacher begins to sing his words and the organist accompanies him as he is beginning to reach a climax in his sermon, whooping is described by John Blake in a 1997 article in *The Atlanta Journal-Constitution* as "traditional Black preaching that relies on voice inflection and vivid storytelling." He said it is "a misunderstood art form, a blend of poetry, parables, and pyrotechnics," the latter because whooping is like the fireworks at the end of the national anthem. But to really understand whooping, you have to fracture it into its parts. Like the vamp in a song, there is repetition in cadence and in words. It's rhythmic, nearly like its own song, and some organists will join in between words, growls, shouts, or exclamations to emphasize inflection points like the soundtrack to a movie, if it's that kind of church service. There is the call and response that is inevitable, because congregants get caught up in the rhythm and begin to urge the preacher on. Then, there are the inevitable antics that come with the expression. There can be a lot of yelling and screaming too, or as Southern detractors might call it, "hootin' and hollerin'," but as E. Dewey Smith, pastor of House of Hope in Atlanta, Georgia, once described it in a 2010 CNN report on the topic, it is "delivering and celebrating the message in a musical style. It's a call and response kind of synergy, and it's really jazz. It's almost an improvisation between the pulpit and the pews."

The preacher becomes so caught up in his message and the flow of the whoop that what some would call showmanship begins to emerge.

I remember an elder mother in the church at Good Street describing how Dr. Clark once in his early preaching years became so enraptured in his whoop while preaching at a small church in the country that had no central air or heating and only had about fifteen rows of pews that he ran down the aisle and out the door, only to emerge seconds later with his head through one of the open windows to whoop at the congregation—and of course the congregants went into a frenzy. At least, that's how the legend goes. This is all alleged, but quite believable.

That was long before my time, but I did witness him wiping his brow with "a handkerchief the size of a bedsheet," as my Aunt Jackie called it—all in the midst of a whoop. He was about five feet, two inches tall, but for a moment there, he seemed to completely disappear behind the huge white cloth only to reemerge with a growl or another whoop. It was unbelievable how he managed to throw his leg over the railing of the pulpit when he was really into his preaching because his legs were so short. How did his leg reach? This was not only astounding, but it was just plain entertaining. So, there was definitely a physicality and showmanship to the art of whooping. Some preachers might run across the platform, but many of them found themselves in the congregation itself. I witnessed the great Melvin Von Wade, pastor of the Mount Zion Missionary Baptist Church in Los Angeles, California, run to the front row of the congregation at the Concord Church in Dallas, Texas, in the early 2000s. He leaped onto the pew between preachers and elders, then stood atop the narrow back of the pew as if it were a balance beam. He was standing with both feet on the pew back, which was less than an inch wide, but balancing all in one fluid and spectacular motion nonetheless. He stood there and delivered another thirty seconds of his whoop to a crowd that left their seats to shout and, in so doing, were able to get a better look at what really happened. Clearly, he wasn't new to this. The preachers around him were in shock, but ultimately, fell out in awe and laughter, shouting him on. They didn't help him up there, because it happened in a flash, but they definitely helped him down.

Young and Old Take More Than Sermon Notes from the Pulpit in the Black Church

It's very common for a family member to bring you to church as a child, even if that family member isn't your own parent. Adrion Porter's first recollection of attending church was from around the age of seven; his grandmother ensured that he and his cousins always attended Sunday School at the New Macedonia Baptist Church in Memphis, Tennessee. This was the same church his father would eventually take over as pastor. His mother and father were divorced at the time, so he shuttled between New Macedonia and the Pleasant Grove Baptist Church.

If you asked him where his speaking skills came from, he'd say that they sprang from his time in church and a long lineage of pastors in his family. Porter is the founder of Mid-Career Mastery, a consultancy for organizations and their mid-career and seasoned talent. He spends the majority of his time speaking on platforms and facilitating workshops and seminars when he isn't writing and developing learning curriculum for executives.

In the survey I conducted with Black leaders, 56 percent said that they'd learned public speaking, presenting, or teaching skills in the Black Church. Adrion Porter is one of those leaders.

To say that he was influenced by what he saw in the pulpit of the Black Church is an understatement. When I asked him about his first time speaking in church, he not only described it, he recalled the entire speech word for word and his interaction with the congregation. While his first memory of church was around the age of seven, Porter was typically an onlooker until he went away to college and returned. That's when his mother suggested that he welcome the visitors during the morning worship service.

"I just didn't want to do only the standard," Porter said. "I needed to put some flair into it, and so I decided to make an acronym out of the word *visitors*. I wanted to stand out and do something that was captivating."

As he recounted this pivotal moment in his life to me, without skipping a beat, he launched into the speech:

> Thank you so much for attending Cumming Street Baptist Church. My name is Adrion. We hope you enjoy our service. And, even though you may consider yourself a visitor, I don't want you to just think of yourself just as a visitor. I'd like to break down that word *visitor* for you. The *V* is for the victory that you will feel in today's message. The *I* is for the invitation that you will have into our community. The *S* is for the spirit and actually the service, the chance for you to serve and to be served. The other *I* is for the inspiration you're going to receive throughout service. The *T* is for the transformation, both personal and spiritual. The *O* is for the openness and the opportunity for growth and connection. The *R* is for the reflection in your spiritual journey. And the *S* is for the spirit you have.

"I still remember to this day!" he said. "And everyone would start clapping," he recalled. "They stood up, and people were like, 'Hey, man!' And all the elders were like, 'All right! Go ahead, young man!' and the ladies, the ushers, [as well as] my mom—she was out there just cheering."

Porter says he was either twenty-two or twenty-three at the

time, and it was the first time he'd ever experienced a congregation respond to him that way. It was not only encouraging but also inspiring to him. Until that point, he'd considered himself a bit of an introvert. Experiences like these shape even his current business as a facilitator and speaker. Today, his highly branded curriculum and keynote messages within Mid-Career Mastery use acronyms, alliteration, vivid storytelling, and even flagging, where a speaker enumerates or "flags" each point one by one. Flagging is a core characteristic of a good expository sermon in the Black Church. It is also what speaking and communications experts say are important platform tools so that an audience will not only recall your points better, but also lean in and be entertained along the way.

Porter didn't exactly dream this style up, but on reflection he realized that he'd been hearing preachers do it since he was a young boy, and it inspired him to be creative, to be authentically himself when it was his time to stand at the podium and welcome the visitors in a way that this particular congregation hadn't heard before. Yet, it seemed very familiar to the crowd because he nearly preached the welcome. It was a mini sermon!

"The associate pastor, Gary Faulkner, was younger, but he had a speaking and preaching style that really captured me," Porter reflected. "He was a very captivating speaker. And I probably was inspired by him. And then the remaining of it, I would say sixty to seventy percent of it, was just me."

He also gave credit to the congregation, known to be warm to first-time speakers, especially young people; this sentiment was echoed by many of the leaders I spoke to about their first experiences standing before church audiences large and small.

Our Brains Love a Well-Told Story

If you'd like for your team to remember something, tell a story. If you want your employee base to be inspired, tell a story. Seems fairly straightforward, but neuroscience research reveals just how powerful storytelling can be for our brains. According to a report by Human Capital Innovations, there are three theories in neuroscience about storytelling and why humans have such an attraction to it. The first is that stories bring meaning to chaos in our minds. The sequencing causes certain neurons to fire off, causing the hippocampus to grow. That's when learning happens. You could very easily share a string of letters and numbers, for instance, those on a dollar bill. There are about thirteen in the series. Most people can't simply glance at them and then rattle them back by memory. However, if you took that same string of numbers and letters and told a story with each letter or number, chances are that most people would remember the stream. Theory two: our brains can simulate social interaction and "broadcast" the images of the story in our minds, allowing us to connect with others better. Our brain is hardwired to imagine in pictures; it craves stories. Share more stories with people, and watch how they lean in.

The third theory in neuroscience research about our brain's affinity to storytelling is that the brain's sensors are stimulated with storytelling. The auditory cortex fires off signals based on sounds, and the sensory cortex begins imagining the sights, smells, movement, and even tastes within the story. This simulation within the mind's eye is extremely intoxicating, and it causes people to feel like they're there, especially when the storyteller is good at their craft.

Perhaps this is why when I saw those yellow jonquils on the Lego box, I recalled the images of pastures full of yellow flowers my childhood pastor had spoken of so eloquently. Stories tap into our primal desire for narrative. Storytelling is how Black people have kept centuries of history and legend in their culture. It's safe to say that storytelling lives within many cultures that center community, generation over generation. While all of humankind can trace oral storytelling back centuries, for Black people in America the ritual of storytelling is particularly significant. Not only did it provide us with a way to preserve our history, recipes, rituals, and traditions, it also provided us with a voice in a society that largely muted us. The Black Church evolved as one of those safe havens for this particular kind of storytelling, and because the Black Church also provided a place to lead when leadership opportunities outside of its walls in the United States were so scarce or nonexistent for Black people, many young people, young adults, and even grown people realized their first opportunity and sometimes only opportunity to lead; most often that chance meant teaching or speaking.

Learning to Act and Look the Part

When I first met Xavier Williams, he was one of the top executives at AT&T, president of their government business. The meeting was a phone call, and in that call I recognized the rhythm in the way he spoke. Most executives, especially on first meeting or when connecting by phone, delivered a tone and tempo that was more stoic and measured. His corporate conversation had notable swagger, but was still professional. He has since retired from the telecom giant; he now sits atop Network Wireless Solutions (NWS) as chief executive. His leadership style is understated and ultracool, which wasn't simply derived from his membership in the Black Greek letter organization Kappa Alpha Psi. I was not surprised when I learned that Xavier had a deep connection with the Black Church, reaching back to his first recollections as an eight-year-old boy. In his day-to-day life he stayed connected to the Black Church because his wife, Apostle Tina Williams, was the pastor of LOV Nation Church in the Dallas–Fort Worth metroplex. You know, sometimes that swagger you see reminds you of a preacher, and I guess I wasn't the only one who caught that vibe from him in the workplace.

"A white guy from Philly walked up to me after I spoke and said, 'Man, that was great! You're a great orator. You remind me of a preacher, a Black preacher,'" Williams recalled with a chuckle. "And it's so funny how a lot of folks outside of the Black community, if you are an articulate Black man, you're either equated to a preacher or a politician. And over the years, I've been called that many different times by well-intentioned people who didn't mean any harm in it, but that was their frame of reference."

This vibe that Williams exudes isn't only about the way he talks and the way he delivers on the platform; it is also about the way he dresses. When asked about the impact the Black Church had on his speaking ability, he was quick to point out that whether consciously or unconsciously, he was inspired and influenced by the Black preacher in the way that he or she delivered their message or even the way the messenger was dressed. It was the first person he could ever recall watching speak to an audience in that capacity.

"By definition, typically, the pastor, the preacher, was one of the most powerful people in your community, and most well respected. You, to a certain extent, held them to a higher standard. *They* held *you* to a higher standard."

He also understood that with this towering influence of the preacher figure, the institution of the Black Church produced an entire package; when leaders emerge from it, the influence is a good one. He was keenly aware as a boy, as a young man, and even as the top executive he is today that he had to remember who he was and "whose" he was. Being "a Williams," a family whose identity was deeply tied to the church experience, meant that there were expectations. That meant decorum, articulation, and the way you behaved and dressed were all a part of the experience. For Williams, the preacher was his first role model. As an executive, he began to notice this same swagger in the Black men that he admired in the corporate realm.

"I grew up watching Ken Chenault. I grew up watching folks like Stanley O'Neill, and what I always observed from them was that their delivery was so smooth. Ken Frazier from Merck... they were just so smooth. When I worked at AT&T, there were a couple of guys, Ray Robinson, Curt Fields, Ray Wilkins, they were always [smooth], and they were always in their Sunday best."

My father was one of the first Black men to reach the highest levels of civil service in the federal government. He was a GS-15 before he retired; he was featured in *Ebony* magazine when I was ten years old. His church suits were also his work suits, three-piece with a gold pocket watch, French cuffs and cufflinks, snappy ties with matching pocket squares. If he showed up at my university, I would always hear from some student that my father was on campus, and "he looked like he meant business," they would say. Either that, or they asked me if he was a preacher.

Performance and Praise Produce Endorphins

Standing before the congregation meant that you needed to look good and perform well, no exceptions. Many Black executives told me that for them, performing well began with their very first Easter speech, at least the one they could remember. Many children in the Black Church began to stand before the congregation the minute they started to babble, even if their parents had to hold them up to the microphone to say their two words, wiping the dribble from their noses or mouths first.

"Dappy Easder!!" they'd say.

"Aaaaaa-MEN!" the congregation would respond.

Williams shared that one of the first experiences he could recall happened during Sunday School, but the most memorable was on Easter Sunday, and that was all about the delivery, the look, and elocution.

"You have to be able to say the Bible verse. Then it was actually reading the Bible verse during youth day and all that good stuff," he said. "My mother is an educator. And it is important in our household to enunciate every word. So it wasn't just about church. It was practicing what you were going to say and being able to enunciate it correctly."

Always resistant to being out front, I stood up and *read* my Easter speech at the age of eight as a means of silent protest. This was a huge no-no, not to memorize and deliver it, and I knew it. It was my way of telling my parents never to put me up to it again unless they wanted to be embarrassed. I probably did an Easter speech three times in my life. The third speech would be the last, but I did like to teach Sunday School when I was provided the opportunity once a month at the early age of fourteen.

Easter speeches aren't unique to the Black Church, but they represent a different and unique opportunity for Black children. Historically, the Black Church represented that one safe venue where Black children could stand up before people and lead and speak; other venues in society silenced, erased, ignored, or passed over Black children, depriving them of similar opportunities. The Black Church has been a safe space for many Black adults as well. When leadership roles seemed to be reserved for the people who didn't look like you at work, you could always step up and lead in the Black Church.

Grammy-nominated singer/songwriter David Frazier, most notable for his single "I Need You to Survive," which became a Black Church anthem in the early 2000s as recorded by Hezekiah Walker, told me that culturally, Black people simply haven't had access to all the venues where their children could step up and have the spotlight. He has recorded more than one hundred songs in the Black Church tradition and currently serves as worship pastor at Shiloh Church in Jacksonville, Florida.

"Whereas culturally, we don't have access to all of the venues, I think there is an intrinsic need to also be heard sometimes, and I think the church allowed us to be heard," he said. "It gives us a platform to express ourselves and be heard, and a safe space. We don't have access to those spaces. I think we have more access to the spaces now, but . . . I think the church satisfied that for a while for people and helped people decide which way they wanted to go and things they wanted to do. And if they ever have a chance to have the microphone again during their matriculation through life, they will then fall back on these experiences."

The boost in confidence that many children receive from learning to perform before an audience is profound, and it prepares them for life's big stage. When a child musters up the courage to stand up before an audience or congregation, she or he is also signaling the brain to fire off endorphins, which trigger a feeling of happiness. In the Black Church, children get to speak, act, sing, or dance.

In an article titled "Spotlight on Confidence: The Science Behind Stage Presence," Deanna Gillian cites a 2008 study called "The Impact of Arts Education on Cognitive and Non-Cognitive Outcomes," which showed that engaging in performing arts, especially at a young age, has a profound impact on brain development.

"When your kids act out a sketch or belt out a tune, their brains are firing on all cylinders," Gillan writes. "It's like a mental workout that flexes creativity, memory, and problem-solving muscles." Building these muscles as a child has incredible implications for adulthood when professionals are at times called on to give a presentation or speech. For some children whose parents aren't able to afford theaters and programs, these skills are learned at church. These skills can be learned at school if a child elects to be a part of theater or speech classes or the choir, but in speaking with Black leaders, they recalled that they received their earliest experience of public speaking before they were school-age at their church. There is something about the tradition of being expected to perform on the platform; it's a mandatory rite of passage, and a child immediately receives strong affirmations from a congregation. In schools and in extracurricular programs, children are passed the mic, in most cases, only if they show interest.

I witnessed this recently at a local church that boasts a roster of some ten thousand members; for two services each Sunday the balconies and overflows are packed. The congregation of this megachurch was predominantly Black, but now the church increasingly hosts people of many backgrounds, including white congregants. Over the years the church has started to include rituals of the Black Church experience. One Sunday in particular stands out in my mind, when the children's leaders stepped onto the platform with three children after the praise team concluded their set. One of the children, a little girl, no more than six years old and missing teeth, stepped up to the microphone and told us that she would be reciting the books of the New Testament, but that she would be doing it in a song.

She stood there and belted out her singsongy version of the twenty-seven books, beginning with Matthew and ending with Revelation. By about the tenth book, the congregation, all 4,500+ members in this particular service, started clapping to the beat and cheering her on. She never flinched, and when she finished, the entire congregation roared in jubilation with a standing ovation. The video remains on YouTube today with more than twelve thousand views and counting. This little girl will never forget that moment, and when everyone started to clap while she sang, her eyes visibly lit up. I thought to myself at that moment that there are some adults who will never get this opportunity to stand before thousands, kill it, and then get a standing ovation . . . anywhere, and this little angel got the experience of proving herself in "big church" with the adults, where you're treated like a little person, empowered on the same platform as adults, and she did it in two services that morning. She's ready for the boardroom, or Broadway . . . either one.

Xavier Williams believes that these traditions have served Black leaders well, but we may have overlooked their true benefit and significance. What could the benefits of this kind of tradition be for Black people outside of the church, particularly in business?

"I think from a transformational standpoint in society in general . . . there's a shift going on where some of the things that we take for granted, we're finding that they were actually very much needed and it wasn't a throwaway," Williams added. "It was something that was a key to the veracity of our entire society and entire community."

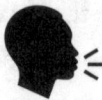

THE LEADERSHIP LESSONS

Master the art of storytelling—it's a leadership superpower. Great leaders are great storytellers. Neuroscience research shows that stories help the brain process information, create meaning from chaos, and stimulate engagement. Use storytelling to communicate complex ideas, inspire teams, and build connections. Incorporate visual language, rhythm, and repetition to make your message memorable.

Develop your delivery style with a commanding presence. Speaking with confidence, rhythm, and authority in combination with strong executive presence influences how people perceive your leadership. Consider your tone, pacing, and body language. Develop a signature speaking style that commands attention without sacrificing authenticity and substance.

Teach what you know to others—it strengthens your leadership. Teaching, mentoring, and guiding others are core to solid leadership. Teach others in your field. Whether it's mentoring, leading training sessions, or speaking at industry events, sharing your knowledge builds credibility, positions you for more opportunities, raises your visibility, and strengthens your leadership skills.

Build your confidence with public speaking opportunities. Speaking publicly—whether in a church, boardroom, or conference—triggers endorphins that reduce anxiety and boost confidence. The more you experience high-pressure communication, the better you'll become at it. Seek out public speaking opportunities, even in small settings. Confidence is built through practice, and the praise you receive reinforces that. Volunteer to lead meetings, present ideas, or host discussions in and out of your professional setting.

Look the part—your personal brand starts with presence. In business, presentation matters. Be polished, poised, and prepared. How you present yourself visually, verbally, and emotionally influences how people receive your message. Be intentional about your presence. Ensure your appearance, speech, and demeanor align with your leadership goals and professional aspirations.

COACHING QUESTIONS

What can you take away from the Black preacher in your quest to become a better speaker?

How might you approach storytelling differently after reading about the Black Church tradition?

What might you do to integrate more performance into your leadership in order to benefit from the happiness triggers?

What best practices in speaking, storytelling, or performance can you glean from the Black Church that might impact the next generation of Black leaders?

4
RESILIENCE
A Balm for the Burden

How would you feel if you went on a company outing with your husband and the bus left you at the venue on the return trip home? This is exactly what happened to Trudy Bourgeois early in her career, and she was mortified. She's a retired equity strategist to the Fortune 500, an author, and a former senior corporate executive. In the early 1990s, she was the only Black leader on an outing to the Kentucky Derby. The coordinators provided instructions about what the participants should do on their way to and from the venue, but just to be clear, Trudy asked the coordinator for the exact time the bus would leave the venue and from what spot the bus would leave to head back to the hotel after the race and events concluded. The coordinator told her the bus would leave at 3:00 p.m. and provided her with the location. Trudy and her husband timed their walk back to the designated stop fifteen minutes earlier than the call time just to be certain they didn't miss the bus. All dressed up in their derby best, the couple arrived at the stop as planned.

"So, we got back early, quite literally because of that principle that I'd learned about honoring each other in terms of time and the way you treat people," Bourgeois said. "But when we got back at 2:45 p.m., this beautifully decorated bus was nowhere to be found. I immediately thought it was my fault because the derby is run in a coliseum. And so, we then rushed to the other side to make sure we were still there by three o'clock. We got to the other side and, of course, no bus." Trudy then called the coordinator and asked where to find the bus, only to learn that it was currently five miles from the coliseum with everyone on board except her and her husband.

"I ugly cried," Bourgeois said.

Although she had told me this story once before, I could still hear the trembling in her voice when she retold it decades later. These were people she worked with; they knew she and her husband were on that bus on the way to the derby. These people made no effort to ensure that she and her husband were on the bus when it was time to return. No one discussed head count. No one looked for them in the restrooms. As the only Black people on the excursion, they would have been hard to miss. She was devastated, but what did she do?

"We caught a cab, went back to the hotel, and went to the CEO's house that night for a cocktail party. Mike didn't want to go. He was furious. He was absolutely, absolutely furious," she said.

"No, we have to go, and we have to present ourselves," she told her husband. "And it happened that the CEO's wife opened the door when we arrived. She took one look at me and knew that I wasn't right. I was visibly broken."

Of course, her boss apologized to her publicly, swearing he had no clue how this could have happened, but the hurt was still there and would be. She felt the ultimate rejection of her person. It felt personal, and she knew in her soul that it probably was.

"But I did what I saw my parents and grandparents do. I moved on," she said. "And in corporate America, if you ruminate, if you let people get into your spirit, it's going to crush you."

It's the story of our lives as Black people. We take the hits and keep on moving forward despite it all, generation over generation; but where do we find it in us to just "move on," as Trudy did, as our parents did, as our grandparents and their ancestors before us did?

Trudy said she learned these lessons of resilience in the Black Church with her grandparents, whom she lovingly called Day and Di. They lived next door and attended the small-frame Baptist church down the hill from her home in segregated Mobile, Alabama. Mobile's population includes many Catholic Creole people. Her parents took her most Sundays to their parish up the hill, St. Ignatius Catholic Church, where they were among the few Black parishioners. She told me she most enjoyed walking to the Christian Union Missionary Baptist Church with her grandmother, who donned big, beautiful hats with matching suits and shoes, because that was the church where the people looked like them, and they invited her and her siblings to actively participate in the worship services and ministries. Trudy and her siblings even formed a band at their grandmother's request, despite Trudy's admission that she wasn't a singer.

She knew from an early age that she had to be tough, and she knew exactly why. As a young girl going to school in the Jim Crow South, she had been called nigger by a young white boy; she continued to go to school because there wasn't a choice. She would learn that work wasn't much better than the schoolyard, and the many stories that her parents and grandparents shared were traumatic. But there they were, still standing, and dressed to the nines while doing so. The church taught her resilience as she watched others manage conflict and adversity both within the church and beyond its doors.

Witnessing the elders in the church, especially her grandparents, refuel to face a hostile world helped her develop an understanding of the kind of resilience needed in the corporate environment.

"When you think about some of the top skills that are needed in the business world, decision-making, communications, agility, and emotional intelligence, [they] were found at that little Baptist church," she said.

Church Trauma Is Also a Source of Pain, Resilience, and Lessons in Conflict Management

Trudy mentioned that in the Black Church she learned how to get along with people; it was necessary because there was always conflict. When you serve in ministry, there is politics, whether you are aware of it or not. There were big fish and little fish, and there were unwritten rules. Some were grasping for power, while others had power simply due to a birthright that someone or some group thrust on them because of their family's standing in the community or their deep pockets. There were those families, those "sacred cows," if you will, that everyone knew wielded some degree of influence, certain rings you must kiss, and there were others who wanted you to pucker up to their backsides instead. Depending on where you found yourself in that political system, life in church could be a pleasure or a pure pain. Doing the business of the church at the church was not for the faint of heart.

At my home church in Dallas, Good Street Baptist Church, I never felt like I was a part of the creamy center, although my family had been members for several decades. My family's position in the church could be described as well-liked and respected. We'd passed the figurative likeability tests, and our social clout passed muster based on my mother and father's status in the community as hardworking people with respectable careers. Rolling up in the right car didn't hurt either, according to the unwritten rules. Mind you, our pastor wasn't the kind to pull up in a Rolls Royce like others might, so that really set the tone. It was a middle-of-the-road luxury car market in the parking lot. Cadillacs were plentiful. If you could roll up in a 1998 Oldsmobile, you were in. We had a burgundy one. Our close family friends had a Delta 88. Foreign luxury cars were nearly nonexistent until the mid-1990s when members of my generation went away and did well for themselves and came back to the city on holiday.

Although the Smith family was aligned correctly with members of the trustee board and the pastor, and Daddy was installed as a deacon and worked closely with the pastor on some business and technology matters, I still considered my family to be outsiders. After all, there were only two generations represented, and that was the makeup of my tiny nuclear family. Until my sister married a son of another family in the church, we had no real blood ties. Good Street was one of those churches that had grands, great-grands, aunts, uncles, cousins, and in-laws and outlaws, all so complex that it's fair to say I'm still learning to this day about all the connections. When my daughter was born, I felt like my parents had reached "elder" status, although not in any official capacity. Their generation was considered the bedrock of the congregation.

I didn't really get my first dose of church trauma until I was a married young adult, and I naively took my marital issues to the leadership at a different church that I'd joined. I remained at that different church for about eighteen months, just long enough for it to get messy. Later, I was glad to bid it all farewell. Some of the trauma I experienced was auxiliary because it happened with a singing group associated with that church, not exactly based there. It was the first gospel group I ever sang with. I was recruited; I didn't know anyone in the group before I joined. It was the first time I met a grown-up mean girl and some messy men who had found their tribe within an ensemble. I also met my first inappropriate pastor during that time. A complete control freak, he was battling demons I wouldn't become aware of until after my near scrape with him. Even his wife at the time admitted to struggling to deal with him. While he was a solid teacher, he fancied himself a counselor as well, which was ill-advised. In a closed-door, one-on-one session he offered to pick me up from the airport on my return from a business trip that I had only mentioned in passing. He also offered me money. I was supposed to be seeing him for marital counseling.

"Do the trustees know that you're offering me this kind of assistance?" I asked him point-blank and without blinking. "As long as that 5 Series is parked outside, I'm employed at my platinum-collar job, and James E. Smith is my father, I will never require any assistance of the sort from you. And if your trustees don't know you're offering this, I will be happy to inform them."

This was my first time shaking a table without actually shaking one, eye-to-eye with a powerful figure. I would definitely take that lesson with me into the boardrooms. The other lesson was if I needed a counselor in the future, I would seek a professional one or a therapist outside of the church. This pastor flapped his gums so badly that congregants approached me with information that could have only come from him. My soon-to-be ex-husband and I found common ground comparing notes on him, even when we generally weren't speaking. It was the one thing we could agree on: this pastor was a slime bucket. Years later, I learned that this pastor got caught up in scandal, had to undergo drug rehab, and ultimately, the then-first lady filed for divorce. Had I done my homework on him, I would have learned that he fell from grace at the church where I would ultimately land next, and where his name was mud with so many of the people there. I would be a member of that next church for seventeen years. While it wasn't without its own brand of trauma, my parents taught me that church-hopping is just not something that the Smiths do. We stay, and we move past it because our focus is on the Lord, not the people. The church was a hospital for sinners, after all, not a hospice for saints, as one of my pastors put it.

Thankfully, I knew how a church was supposed to work because I had witnessed it from birth at Good Street. I saw how a pastor should carry himself, so that one trying instance didn't sour me on the church, as a whole. It isn't always like that for others. In fact, one reason that many millennials and Gen Zers abbreviate their church attendance or stop it completely is because of situations like this— bum pastors, betrayals, and in my opinion, gossip. But for those of us who stay despite it all, there is an opportunity for personal and leadership development.

Running into that disliked colleague in the hallways or elevator at work is not the dilemma it could be; when you've matriculated from the B-school (the Black Church), you're set. In small to medium-sized churches like the one I grew up in, there was no avoiding a person in the hallway. I've seen that happen in very human ways. Two people that have an issue see each other in the halls, and the urge to tell them where to go takes over. I've even seen it come to blows—yes, even at church. Handbags and Bibles flying. But you learn. You learn to see that person across the room on a regular basis, and you learn forgiveness or at least develop a thicker skin. Maybe not immediately, but eventually. You can't forget because that person is *still* in the pews, *still* in the ladies' lounge, *still* doing the morning announcements—until that one day you find yourself co-chairing Women's Day together. You just have to figure it out and move forward or brace for the mess. Either way, you make it through, and you learn a lesson.

In modern-day megachurches, it's a little easier to plan the avoidance. You can go to the early service if they go to the late one, but if you plan to lead and participate in ministry and they do too, you will likely still have an occasion to work with them. When you consider it, it's a healthy dynamic, like when someone in your family crosses you, do you generally run out on them? No. In healthy families, you learn to work it through.

Resilience Is a Burden and a Blessing

Search out any definition of *resilience* in modern leadership books, and you will discover that resilience comes at a cost. The price you pay, typically through adversity, failure, or even trauma, is what grants you admission to an exclusive club of resilient people. Those who have not suffered much have low resilience and must practice risk-taking in order to reap resilience's blessings. Resilience brings with it the burden of having withstood adversity and sometimes trauma and can lead to an emotional toll if we don't intentionally seek to heal. This can be especially true for Black people who have suffered generation after generation; the trauma is etched onto our very DNA, which is called epigenetics. Resilience is also a reward—a superpower. It allows us to see the next obstacle juxtaposed with the previous one and others in the past, and chances are we've fought off even bigger demons in the past, which prepares us for future battles.

Trudy said that her experience at the Kentucky Derby left an indelible mark on her, a scar no less, but it was a battle scar that reminds her how to show up despite what may have just happened. It allows people to wear a poker face or sometimes a pleasant smile in the corporate towers and boardrooms, places where prejudices can be quite intense. These are the times that try the souls of more privileged men and women—but not the battle-scarred, high-performing Black leader.

This resilience is a passport to emotional intelligence, a critical trait in leadership that helps us to manage conflict, build self-awareness, and read the room and the emotions of others, according to the American Psychological Association (APA). The organization defines resilience as "the process of adapting well in the face of adversity, trauma, tragedy, threats, or significant sources of stress." It also helps leaders to recover from setbacks. It's that epic bounce back we see in some of the best leaders. It can also lead to extraordinary personal growth, including but not limited to granting access to a growth mindset when we look for the lesson in adversity. Self-reflection is key. Asking yourself, "What did I learn from this situation?" can unlock a world of problem-solving abilities and insights that can lead to a more powerful influence with others.

The Black Church Is Where Coping Strategies Blossom

"Your setback is a setup for a comeback!" I've heard many preachers proclaim this from the pulpit and was never sure where it originated. I just know that when I was going through setbacks at home or at work, a good word from on high or an inspirational song from the choir was just what the doctor ordered to refuel me on Sunday before going back into the mean streets of corporate America on a Monday morning. My church was where my "Sunday evening scaries" came to die. I'd take them right to the altar and leave them there. When I learned of impending layoffs at the big company nearly a year before my pink slip actually arrived, I wasn't shaken. Despite a boss that had it out for me, I knew that half the battle was showing up with dignity and continuing to perform in a way that not only represented my own brand but also my family's name and my faith. My mother taught me from a very young age something that her mother passed down to her and her siblings: "Always remember who you are and *Whose* you are." She always called attention to the capital letter in *Whose*, for the word had a double meaning. It was as much about representing the family as it was about being one of the Almighty's children—a theme reenforced Sunday after Sunday, Wednesday night after Wednesday night, Watch night after Watch night. We sang that we were "in the Lord's Army" in vacation Bible school, with the word as our sword and the breastplate of righteousness as our protection. It followed that we should also dress the part. So during tough times, I was even more pulled together than when the road was less rocky. The hair was near perfection. The nails, always manicured. The shoes, polished and unscuffed. Once, a nemesis at one firm where I worked said I had "First Lady" hair, you know, referring to the other, more-famous Michelle. Still others commented on the grace I exuded even when the corporate darts were flying and even as they hit the target. We also learned to look and be unaffected, and this wasn't too difficult, because the reality was that we often had faced bigger obstacles before, at home, at work, maybe even at church. Our value was drilled into us in the Black Church in ways it wasn't in other places in the world. Yes, at school you may have been offered the chance to lead your class or your league or in school sports, but if you were in an environment that *othered* you and centered whiteness, you may have experienced the same neglect or vitriol you would eventually face at work.

The day I met Trudy Bourgeois, I began to suspect that the lessons we learned in the Black Church were threading the needle of a narrative for high-performing Black leaders in the highest echelons of business. She was facilitating a leadership cohort that I was a part of, and I will never forget what she said, because I'd never been in a professional environment where a spiritual statement was so boldly proclaimed. While she was reminding a room full of Black women leaders to know our value, she made this statement: "Remember that you are a daughter of God." I was stunned. Never had I ever experienced my church life overlapping with my professional life so palpably. Yes, we were taught to take what we learned on Sunday into Monday through Friday, but we were told to hide this in our hearts. The corporate culture doubled down on the idea that we should keep our faith to ourselves, but it was okay to live by it. Even the corporate values of ethical leadership aligned with it, but never should it be discussed. Generations before us received their weekly dose of resilience in church, but it wasn't always because of the lessons taught and songs sung. My eighty-one-year-old parents lived through Jim Crow in the South and the Civil Rights Movement, and the Black Church was not only a refuge, it was a headquarters for the movement.

According to the 2020 National Institutes of Health (NIH) report called "Black Resilience—Broadening the Narrative and the

Science on Cardiovascular Health and Disease Disparities," Black American populations have the ability to overcome traumas, societal and environmental adversities, and more because of individual and collective resilience that resulted from their history of oppression. Despite the devastating toll of the Jim Crow South, Black people in America reaped a superpower that is quite unique to them—an abundance of resilience.

The blurred lines in defining resilience may be best addressed within a "multiple resiliencies" framework that explains how an individual can combine their psychological resilience with other types of resilience (e.g., physiological, social) to achieve a physical resilience in the face of biological stressors, internal and external. For Blacks, instances of health and longevity co-exist with terrible disparities, the latter of which are "utterly predictable," given the strains borne disproportionately by Blacks.

So, resilience in humans can be psychological, social, and physiological. The report highlights a phenomenon in the Black community, what psychologists call social cohesion. It is the bond that is formed when a group of people have a shared experience, especially rooted in adversity, that causes them to gravitate toward each other and find a common purpose. In fact, this kind of purpose in life that Black leaders find in church has cardiovascular benefits. The research provides strong evidence that social cohesion gives us healthy hearts because attributes like "purpose in life" are powerful predictors of cardiovascular health and resilience in Black communities.

According to research from MinistryWatch, an independent

organization that provides information about Christian ministries and advocates for donors, the Black Church has historically served as a cornerstone of emotional and communal resilience through involvement in ministries and weekly worship. It builds emotional strength and psychological resilience, providing tools that Black professionals carry into the workplace. The organization points to research from Barna Group, a respected research organization that monitors culture and Christianity over time and that informs many faith-based institutions. It reported in a recent article called "Most Black Adults Say Religion and the Black Experience Go Hand in Hand" that the percentage of Black adults seeing faith as a source of emotional strength dipped only slightly over the past twenty-five years. In 1996, 91 percent of respondents said they rely on the church. By 2020, 87 percent of those respondents felt the same way, representing a decline of only 4 percent. In addition, most said their association with a Black Church provides them with comfort, agency, and emotional strength and "counter[s] a broader sense of political powerlessness."

The empowerment that comes from the Black Church can be viewed in many ways. There is the equipping that happens through training and learning. There is the community that creates power through its alignments and connections, but most distinctly, there is the "powering up" that Black leaders receive in the pews from a good word or even a song.

"The sisters would be swaying in the front pew," Bourgeois recalled. "And as a kid, I'd say, 'What is that?' But what I appreciated was that they were refilling their cups to go back out into the world and deal with a very ugly place that didn't like Black people at all. It was such a source of power."

The Science of Resilience Builds Leaders in the Pews

There are scientific reasons why bathing oneself in the fountain of inspiration builds resilience; inspiration overflows each Sunday from the Black Church, through "going in," or "catching the Holy Spirit," or simply swaying or tapping a toe to the rhythmic A-and-B selections. What is happening is spiritual, but the behavior change begins in the brain with a mindset shift. The notable psychologist Carol Dweck, who is credited with the popular "Mindset Theory" that focuses on growth and fixed mindsets, has researched this phenomenon. In her research she focused on how humans nurture both fixed and growth mindsets through habits and also with what we are presented with in our environment. How we respond to the stimuli in the environment matters most. Growth mindsets are a result of facing adversity; reflecting on the lessons from conflict, pain, or trauma; and nurturing a mind that allows us to face additional adversity. Adversity can help us power through and learn something, even if we fail. Growth mindsets are built when that vamp in the song or that point in the sermon reminds us that what we are going through is only for a season, that "trouble don't last always," and that as long as we are focused with our faith, there is hope for something better. The growth mindset allows us to "get back up again," like the Donnie McClurkin song says, "We fall down, but we get up." Time in prayer and in worship allows us to build that capacity to withstand or to recover quickly from difficulties and makes us tougher. It's the bounce back that we build into our being when we bow our heads, making us more pliable and less breakable. It's the adaptability that provides us a way to achieve long-term success in business and in life.

In *The Gerontologist*, a periodical that focuses on the longevity of older adults, a recent article called "'You Need a Song to Bring You Through': The Use of Religious Songs to Manage Stressful Life Events" explores how older Black people use religious songs to cope with stressful life events. While other neuroscience research demonstrates how stress can actually strengthen resilience when combined with proper emotional regulation and coping strategies, songs in the Black Church seem to be already leveraged for exactly that. Black churchgoers interviewed for the article were using faith singing to cope with stressful life events: "Religion expressed through song was a coping strategy for participants experiencing stressful life events who described feelings of being comforted, strengthened, able to endure, uplifted, and able to find peace by turning to the types of religious songs described here."

The report goes on to note that there are six types of songs that were particularly helpful in building resilience in these Black churchgoers:

- Songs of thanksgiving
- Praise songs
- Instructive songs
- Songs that remind them of ancestors
- Songs that communicate with God
- Songs that explore life after death

Black churchgoers saw benefits from these songs that spoke specifically to hope, inspiration, awe, gratitude, joy, pride, serenity, and love—eight of the ten positive emotions designated by neuroscience as those that will lift a mood, motivate forward motion, and easily eliminate a negative mood. The other two positive effects are interest and amusement, which are typically accessible at the Black Church through its ministries and outreach.

Resilience Is Especially Important to Black Executive Leaders

If resilience had an even more experienced, older, wiser, and tougher cousin, it'd be grit. In her book *Grit: The Power of Passion and Perseverance*, Angela Duckworth describes grit as sustained resilience and passion over time. The Black Church has demonstrated the grit necessitated by generation after generation of steadfastness Black people demonstrated in the midst of historical difficulties, misfortunes, hardships, and distress over the past two centuries. Where else would you sing, "Another day's journey and I'm glad about it"? The Black Church was teaching Black leaders to expect rejection, obstacles, and pain, but to greet these with positivity because of the hope that "trouble would soon be over." Grit is described as the courage, resolve, and strength of character to push through those tough times. Duckworth says that it takes heart. Her work in psychology reveals how leaders who maintain long-term focus despite setbacks are more successful.

Black executive leaders must have this long-term focus, and they know that the higher you climb in business, the more challenging the job becomes. There are several reasons for this:

- The spaces you enter become more exclusive and most often whiter
- Isolation becomes more intense
- The scrutiny becomes even more exacting

Black leaders must enter these narrow spaces with a special additive that bests their competition in environments that question if their being a leader is suitable in the first place. For them, that ingredient is grit. Their competency is questioned when their counterparts' are not. Their authority is contested frequently or they are thrown into crisis situations with the expectation to right sinking ships. In a 2023 *Nonprofit Quarterly* article titled "The Perils of Black Leadership," the author Cyndi Suarez explores how Black leaders, especially women, are frequently appointed during crises—known as "the glass cliff"—and how they are forced to develop or tap into extraordinary resilience to meet or exceed the challenge. Likely one of the most unmistakable examples of this is the 2024 election cycle, when the Democrats urged President Joe Biden to step aside in one of the country's most contentious races for the White House, and Biden tapped Vice President Kamala Harris to become the Democratic presidential nominee. In any other season, her selection would likely not be so significant aside from the historic nature of her run as the first woman of color to be a candidate for president of the United States. At least half of the nation was depending on her to "save democracy." The other candidate for the office was the forty-fifth president of the United States, Donald J. Trump. At that point Trump had racked up thirty-four felony counts, various other criminal charges including sexual assault, and a reputation for racist and misogynistic rants online and off. He had a questionable association with a group called The Heritage Foundation, whose 2025 manifesto called for undoing the Constitution, closing the Department of Education, deporting immigrants, and taking women out of the workforce, sending them back to their homes without a vote. This positioned Harris for the presidential run of her life; at stake were the concerns about the reproductive and civil rights of countless Americans. The stakes were high. The amount of resilience on display during her abbreviated campaign and especially throughout the debate, which many pundits and experts called the best presidential debate performance in our country's history, was extraordinary. Still, naysayers doubted her credentials, her ability, and even her competency despite a glowing track record as a prosecutor, a district attorney, a senator, and the first woman vice president of the United States. Her Tiffany pearl earrings must have been audio devices according to some conspiracy theorists. The network must have slipped her the questions ahead of the debate, said others. Still, some claimed she must have used witchcraft on her opponent to get him off his game. The irony is that the vice president is Baptist. Her naysayers couldn't say they didn't like her policies or admit that they just didn't like her. Her performance excellence was too excellent to be believed. While Trump called for mass deportations and accused Haitian refugees of killing and consuming the local pets in Springfield, Ohio, Harris was outlining her plan for an "opportunity economy."

There's no wonder the first call she made after receiving news from President Biden that he wanted her to run was to her pastor. She requested prayer.

She would definitely need it.

Like a song, prayer is also used as a coping strategy for stressors that improves resilience according to the NIH, and it provides those who believe with a direct connection to a higher power that can trigger positive feelings of peace and happiness despite the challenges Black leaders face.

CALL AND RESPONSE

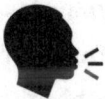

THE LEADERSHIP LESSONS

Wield resilience as a leadership superpower. Leaders who develop resilience can withstand adversity better, learn from failure, and navigate challenges without losing focus. The APA defines resilience as the ability to adapt well in the face of adversity, trauma, or stress. Studies show that resilience enables leaders to recover quickly from setbacks and fosters emotional intelligence, which is critical in managing conflicts and building influence.

Engaging emotional intelligence elevates leadership performance. The ability to manage emotions, both one's own and those of others, is crucial for effective leadership. The emotional quotient (EQ) consists of self-awareness, self-regulation, motivation, empathy, and social skills—all key traits of successful leaders. Neuroscience confirms that resilience strengthens the EQ, allowing leaders to remain composed under pressure.

Cultivate a growth mindset for long-term success. Leaders must embrace a growth mindset, seeing challenges as opportunities to learn and grow rather than as roadblocks. Psychologist Carol Dweck's "Mindset Theory" explains that a growth mindset—believing abilities can be developed through effort—leads to greater achievement. Facing adversity with a mindset of perseverance fosters stronger leadership skills.

Master organizational dynamics to lead with influence. Great leaders understand power structures, navigate unwritten rules, and build influence within their organizations. To lead effectively, observe and analyze the political landscape of your workplace, identify key decision-makers, and strategically align with individuals who drive change. Research in organizational behavior highlights that political skill—the ability to read power dynamics and build relationships—is a key predictor of leadership effectiveness. Leaders who can navigate complex workplace structures, manage competing interests, and leverage influence are more likely to succeed in driving change and advancing their careers.

Leverage mindfulness, reflection, and other introspective coping skills to strengthen leadership. Leaders who cultivate mental and emotional resilience through reflection, mindfulness, and community support are better equipped to handle workplace stress, navigate challenges, and sustain high performance. Research from the NIH confirms that faith-based coping strategies—such as prayer, meditation, and communal support—enhance emotional resilience, reduce stress, and improve decision-making under pressure. Studies also show that leaders who practice mindfulness and intentional reflection develop higher levels of emotional intelligence, which improves their ability to lead effectively.

COACHING QUESTIONS

What are the major lessons from a Black leader's experience with building resilience in the Black Church?

CALL AND RESPONSE

What obstacles have you faced that could have benefited from better resilience in you?

How will you intentionally cultivate resilience as you aspire for better leadership?

Who in your life demonstrates resilience or grit? What is their story? How do you believe they built it?

5
PERSEVERANCE
Learning to Keep on Keeping On

The summer of 2024 was hot here in Texas. We're talking triple-digit heat. But the temperature really heated up across the nation, and likely around the world, when President Joe Biden announced in a letter shared on social media that he would be stepping down as the Democratic candidate for president of the United States. It was shocking to most of the country, although there had been calls from inside the party for him to step aside. Biden seemed defiant and strong-willed about his determination to stay in the race despite a rocky performance at a debate against his controversial Republican opponent. There had even been unofficial chatter about who might replace him on the ticket, and the buzz around that selection was that it was possibly happening at the Democratic National Convention the following month. The other surprise was actually in the letter. Biden boldly endorsed his vice president, Kamala Harris, to take over the top of the ticket in his stead as the Democratic nominee.

What happened next left everyone gobsmacked. Harris galvanized her community after placing a call to her pastor, Rev. Amos C. Brown of the Third Baptist Church in San Francisco, requesting a prayer. Then she collaborated with a network of Black women to mobilize, organize, and raise funds; most of these women were church leaders, sorority members, elected officials, celebrities, and community members. A video call hosted by Win with Black Women began as a call for about one thousand Black women; it quickly mushroomed to a call to more than forty-four thousand. I was one of them. The video platform kept failing until an executive many identified as a Southeast Asian woman called her CEO to see what could be done to accommodate this ever-growing video call. The buzz was that Aparna Bawa, the chief operating officer at Zoom, the video conferencing platform, persevered; that video call became the largest Zoom had ever hosted in its history. It was part prayer meeting, part church service, and part sorority meeting with members from all "Divine 9" sororities in attendance and many of their husbands including sorority members from Alpha Kappa Alpha, of which Harris is a member and so am I. Even more significantly, it racked up more than $1.2 million for Harris's less-than-a-day-old campaign. It stirred up a movement and a string of other spinoff video calls hosted by all sorts of groups—some estimate more than one hundred—over the course of the next month: Win with Black Men, White Women for Harris, Latinas for Harris, AAPIs for Harris, LGBTQ+ for Harris, Christians for Harris, Evangelicals for Harris, Republicans for Harris, Red States for Harris, Swifties for Harris, and more. According to reports, Harris raised more than $500 million in a month's time, smashing campaign records as the most money raised by any candidate for president in that short a time span: $81 million in one day, $200 million in one week according to her campaign reports. Ultimately, she would raise more than $1 billion in her 107-day campaign, the shortest presidential campaign in modern history. Only a day after the Democratic National Convention ended, the campaign reported an additional $82 million raised for the campaign; Zoom announced its new capacity to host up to one million participants.

This incredible push forward wasn't without major headwinds pushing against Harris. There were rumors that behind the scenes the top Democratic heavyweights weren't in favor of her running at all. Her Republican opponent, #45, immediately began misogynistic and racial attacks. Even some segments of the Black community were vocal about their doubts about her candidacy, which would make her the first Black and Asian woman to become the official nominee of a major party ticket, and ultimately, if all went in her favor, the president of the United States. With that one bold and commanding endorsement from President Biden, a prayer with her pastor, and a band of Black women rallying together quickly, the Harris campaign persisted and will no doubt go down in history as one of the most well-executed, shortest, yet most inspiring and hard-fought campaigns in US history.

Harris wouldn't be the first Black candidate for POTUS to have strong ties to the Black Church. In fact, all of them have, beginning with Shirley Chisholm, continuing with Rev. Jesse Jackson, followed by President Barack Obama, who would become #44; like the Jackie Robinson of the White House, Obama was the first Black president of the United States. Chisholm, Jackson, Obama, and Harris displayed a fusion of faith, justice, and community engagement. Add in some extraordinary oratorical skills and that combination seems to be the cocktail for success in what is likely the most demanding, grueling, and awe-inspiring journey to the highest office in the land. It goes without saying that one must persevere to run for president of the United States, but especially as a Black person, where slavery, Jim Crow, and the Civil Rights Movement are the highlights of the community's history in America. The odds of any one person becoming POTUS is minuscule, so try being Black. Thus far, only one of the four Black candidates has made the cut. Chisholm and Jackson never made it onto the top of the ticket. Harris did and Obama did. Obama, obviously, made it to the White House for two terms.

A Legacy of Black Persevering Presidential Hopefuls

When former First Lady Michelle Obama took to the platform at the 2024 Democratic National Convention to make the case for Harris, she made an observation: "America, hope is making a comeback!" No doubt, this was an allusion to her husband's campaign speech and platform, even employing a powerful call and response with the audience with the words "Do something!" This chant was inspired by the words of Kamala Harris's mother, who often told her daughter not to sit around and complain, but to take action. Throughout the speech, Michelle Obama highlighted the importance of active participation and the need to take concrete steps in the face of challenges—the kind of action that puts arms and legs to resilience and turns it into perseverance. As she emphasized the urgency of the upcoming election, she encouraged the crowd to repeat "Do something," energizing the audience to remain proactive in the pursuit of a better future. This moment underscored her message that change requires effort, unity, and a refusal to be passive in the face of adversity, reinforcing the idea that every individual's actions matter in shaping the country's direction.

Michelle Obama's speech definitely took strong cues from her husband's platform as well as some creative and cultural license from the Black Church. President Barack Obama's campaign was deeply rooted in the power of "hope" as a force for meaningful change. His unforgettable 2004 "Audacity of Hope" address and his groundbreaking 2008 presidential run echoed the call-and-response cadence of the Black Church. This rhetorical style wasn't just a technique—it was a bridge, connecting him to diverse audiences and offering a vision of unity and progress. Obama's words carried the spirit of perseverance, reflecting the unwavering belief of the Black Church in faith and community as tools to overcome any obstacle. At the heart of Obama's message was his vision of America as a "Beloved Community," where every person, regardless of background, is treated with dignity and respect. His speeches, rich with scriptural references, embodied a hope that resonated with those who had been shaped by the teachings of the Black Church, reminding them of the transformative power of faith and collective action.

Obama's platform was built on the chassis of Jesse Jackson's, whose 1988 speech heralded a call and response that still rings in the hearts and minds of Americans who remember his refrain: "Keep hope alive! Keep hope alive!" Jackson's presidential campaigns are renowned for their electrifying rhetoric, deeply steeped in the Black Church's traditions. His 1988 Democratic National Convention address stands as a quintessential example of hope intertwined with the spirit of perseverance. In this speech, Jackson championed unity through diversity, referring to the concept of a "rainbow coalition" and honoring the legacy of past civil rights icons like Rosa Parks. This aligns closely with the Black Church's historical commitment to social justice, reinforcing the conviction that collective determination can spark transformative change.

Jackson, being the storied Baptist preacher that he was, leveraged an adept use of biblical references and a distinct oratory style, drawing parallels to the impassioned sermons characteristic of Black churches. His proclamation that "we are standing on someone's shoulders" underscores the unyielding spirit of hope, fueled by the sacrifices and triumphs of Black leaders, many of whom had deep roots within the Black Church.

Harris's run harkened back to the first Black woman to run for the presidency, Shirley Chisholm; themes of perseverance and hope flowed through her messages as well. Drawing on her experience in the Black Church, Chisholm embodied perseverance as she focused her fight on racial and gender barriers. Her iconic slogan, "Unbought and Unbossed," reflected the Black Church's ethos of persevering in faith and conviction despite societal challenges and the isolation of being a historic first. Chisholm's message emphasized hope for an America where everyone's voice would be heard, regardless of their race or gender.

In her acceptance speech at the 2024 Democratic National Convention, Kamala Harris painted a vivid picture of the values instilled in her by her mother. Harris called on themes of hope, perseverance, and even faith—chief among them, the call to serve others and the importance of hope during challenging times. She shared the story of her mother, Shyamala Gopalan Harris, a courageous woman who journeyed from India to the United States at just nineteen with a dream of curing cancer. Despite the immense task of raising Kamala and her sister, Maya, alone, Shyamala ensured they learned powerful lessons of resilience, compassion, and a deep pride in their intertwined Black and Indian heritage.

"My mother taught me that service to others gives life purpose and meaning," Kamala Harris recalled in her acceptance speech.

This principle mirrors the teachings of the Black Church, where service and faith are pillars of the community. She also cited her mother's advice to "walk by faith and not by sight," a powerful biblical lesson rooted in 2 Corinthians 5:7. This message resonates with the Black Church tradition, which often serves as a beacon of hope during uncertain times. Harris's words embody the enduring belief in the transformative power of faith and perseverance, values that guided her journey as a lawyer, district attorney, attorney general, US senator, and vice president of the United States. By sharing her personal narrative, Harris not only honors her mother's legacy but also plants seeds of hope, inspiring others to continue the fight for equality and justice. Perseverance moves resilience to action. Harris wasn't shy about her roots in the Black Church throughout her campaign either; she took the pulpit at the Koinonia Christian Church in Greenville, North Carolina, with less than thirty days to go in the campaign and spoke of the importance of perseverance with faith in action. At the time, North Carolina was in the wake of the devastation of Hurricane Helene, so she took some time to encourage the congregation:

> So, scripture teaches, "Let us not become weary in doing good, for at the proper time we will reap a harvest if we do not give up." So, I first encountered the words of Galatians as a young girl at Twenty-Third Avenue Church of God in Oakland, California, which is where I sang in the children's choir and first learned the teachings of the Bible. My earliest memories of those teachings are about a loving God, a God who asks us to speak up for those who cannot speak for themselves, to defend the rights of the poor and the needy. And so, at an early age, I learned that faith is a verb. It is something

we show in action and in service. And we show it by heeding the words of my pastor, who Bishop spoke with yesterday, Reverend Dr. Amos C. Brown, who often invokes the words that we all know: One must do justice, love mercy, and walk humbly with our God. That truth is important at all times and especially in moments of difficulty and disaster, especially in moments like this, as we navigate storms that have inflicted so much harm across our country."

Hope Powers Perseverance

Perseverance is resilience with feet; however, hope is the spring in its step. It is likely the reason why hope was a recurring theme in each of these presidential candidates' messaging. Each of their campaigns linked to hope as the reason to persevere in the quest to have a nation that looks forward toward fairness, freedom, and equality. This is the theme throughout scripture that powers the preaching and songs within the Black Church that herald the promise of hope for a better life "through many dangers, toils and snares," seen and unseen. Resilience is the first step to perseverance because resilience is who you are after you've been battle tested, bent but not broken. Perseverance is the action you take, the pushing through, the "keep on keeping on" that moves you forward and through the next adversity.

These leadership lessons also found their way into homes, and the influence was undeniable. Renee Horne, a chief marketing officer at one of the world's largest financial institutions, recalls growing up in St. Louis, Missouri, getting baptized at the New Sunny Mount Missionary Baptist Church, and hearing sermons that focused on self-control, obedience, and perseverance, but she also admitted that she saw perseverance modeled through her parents at home before she could even recall the words to any of those sermons. The lives of her parents were the sermon. Her mother worked as a corporate administrative assistant by day and went to school at night to finish her degree. Her father was a member of the military. She said they modeled the principles they learned in church and passed them along to her and her siblings through everyday encounters and simple sayings like "A watched pot never boils, so like faith, you gotta wait on it," or "He may not come when you want Him, but He's always right on time." Both were lessons in patience and the "push through" that it takes to make it in life as well as in work.

"My mother and her siblings grew up in foster homes, and they were traumatized as young children," Horne recalled. "And then, as we grew up under the village of their leadership and their storytelling and their experiences and teachings, they nurtured and poured into us so that we didn't have to make the same mistakes or have the same hurt."

Hopeful people are more likely to set challenging goals according to renowned researcher in positive psychology Martin Seligman. Leaders persist through obstacles and find multiple ways to achieve their goals. Then there is the "Hope Theory," which describes hope as a "life-sustaining human strength" and offers three main aspects to this positive mindset: goal thinking, pathways thinking, and agency thinking. Goal thinking is having clear goals that align with one's values. Pathways thinking allows one to strategize ways to achieve that goal. Agency thinking allows us to believe that we have the ability to act to achieve our goals. All three are grounded in the idea that change and trouble is inevitable, but it also asks, "What will you do about it?" Ultimately, the premise of the theory is that hope is the state of mind that helps us keep moving forward even when times are tough. If hope allows us the ability to look forward beyond challenges, it also inspires anticipation. Anticipation is the understanding that "something good is going to happen to you," the refrain from the theme song I remember ringing out from the staticky television set in our family room when my mother turned the channel to televangelism pioneer Oral Roberts, who brought American Pentecostalism and the beginnings of prosperity gospel doctrine primarily to working-class white people via television in the 1970s. Those facing adversity gravitated to the message and used the hope it produced to press on "anyhow." That message resonated with Black churchgoers as well. It was very similar to hearing Mahalia Jackson belting out tunes on my grandmother's living room record player in a tiny town thirty minutes northeast of Texarkana, Texas, just minutes up the two-lane highway from Hope, Arkansas, known as the home of former president Bill Clinton, and another few minutes and not too far away from a town called Stamps. This is where my grandmother grew up in the same town as Maya Angelou. The long-playing record seemed to be always on repeat in the little wood-framed house in Lewisville, Arkansas. Jackson belted out words like "Gonna lay down my burden / down by the riverside" and "study war no more." This anticipation that she sang of was laced with hope for a better future, in fact, likely an afterlife where she would no longer face adversity. The implication was that the long journey, filled with trouble, would be over sooner or later; and the takeaway from that song was that hope would see her, and anyone singing it, to the end where well-deserved peace and joy abounded.

It isn't lost on me that this song made its way into my grandmother Sapora's home because she'd heard the song in church, perhaps on gospel radio as well; somehow, the Black Church always made it into the home. That was a good thing, because taking your burdens to the Lord didn't only happen in the sanctuary. It happened Monday through Saturday in your life as well, and that is just the point. The perseverance itself was rarely needed in the pews. Perseverance happened the minute the benediction was pronounced, but it was up to you to put that hope that you sang, read, and heard about into action.

Sometimes, that hope guides us to leave the safety of our cushy corporate jobs when they aren't serving us or aligning with our values, and it is the perseverance that results from it that supports us on that road less traveled. However, deeply embedded into the idea of perseverance is the understanding that time is a huge factor. It presses for patience, faith, and endurance.

Former talent executive and leadership consultant Dominique "Dom" Jones said hope and anticipation of something better were exactly what gave him the strength to leave a full-time job at one of the most admired brands in the world. He knew that powering up on perseverance was best for him and would allow him to reach the destination where he could lay down his burden. It was his riverside.

"The final light was when I had a chance to take about six weeks off for paternity leave. That was the first time I had a chance to really pump the brakes, get still, get quiet, get centered," Jones said. "And going back was difficult. It was so difficult. Not even because of the work, but the environment played a big role in that."

Dom reflected on how stepping back and surrendering to divine timing propelled him to make a bold leap. He recognized that he had to let go of what no longer served him, no matter the access to medical coverage and investment accounts. This deep trust in faith, woven tightly with resilience, allowed him to persevere through the uncertainty that lay ahead. He described the intense anxiety of being the sole provider for his family and a sole proprietor, yet despite the palpable fear, he understood that relinquishing the past would carve out pathways to future opportunities. He learned this in the Black Church through the teachings and preachings of church elders like his father, who was a pastor, and also through the songs he sang in the choir and as a worship leader. Perseverance became so much a part of the fabric of who he was, from the time he was a child, that pressing forward in faith ultimately felt to him like a duty, especially because what was on the other side of fear in this instance was something that aligned with his values—more of him for his family, less of him for the demands of work. Dom now makes a living gathering groups of professionals in cohorts to teach them leadership principles grounded in biblical values. He also consults with large organizations that need expertise in talent acquisition and development. Additionally, he supports his wife as they homeschool all three of their young boys, and unlike Lot's wife he was obedient when he heard the call, and he isn't looking back.

Anticipation Makes Us Happier for the Journey

The brain is a complex organ, and it is the main center for our thoughts, beliefs, memory, motor skills, behavior, emotions, and other cognitive functions. Certain triggers can cause a range of neurotransmitters to fire off, but if you tap into anticipation, your brain receives a dopamine hit, which makes a person happy, gives them a positive surge of joy, and ultimately, if it happens frequently, improves mental health and well-being. Forward-looking expectancy, as it turns out, has a more powerful effect on our mood than looking back on great things in the past does. That means we get more excited about the things that haven't even happened yet than the things that have happened and are a reality.

I remember when my work environment became challenging and downright toxic; something that lightened the load was that I was already pondering my next step. As I wrote in *No Thanks: 7 Ways to Say I'll Just Include Myself*, while many use vision boards to dream and envision their next move, I wrote my resignation letter and placed it on the desktop of my company laptop. That was my vision board. The idea wasn't to pull the trigger on that letter and immediately press send, but it was my reminder that I had something to which I could look forward. In the meantime, I was also creating the scenario for my exit by having conversations and interviews with companies I would seriously consider joining. I was building my own business, launching a podcast, and beginning to pitch book ideas to a major publisher. I was also accepting interviews internally, exploring all options, but most of all there was the excitement and expectations I conjured for myself by "leaning on the everlasting arms," as we would sing in church, "trusting in His Holy Word," knowing that "He never failed me yet." I didn't know what was next, but I just knew it was far better than my current situation. So when that surplus notice dropped into my inbox, in January 2019, I greeted that layoff with an audible, joyous squeal. Not only would this chapter in my life be a powerful addition to my story, but I would also get paid to leave if I decided against securing another role within the company. When I'd had enough of the internal interviews to find another role within the company and decided to tell the lead officer of my business unit that I was leaving, it felt so good. It didn't matter that my next steps seemed fuzzy. I recall colleagues panicking about me finding another job before I left, and they were startled by my calm. Having something to look forward to, and while still uncertain what that would be, was almost like a drug—a little bit scary, but what a high knowing that "something good was going to happen" to me. Within a few months, it did. The day after I left that position, I stepped on a plane to head to an HBCU to join former *A Different World* star Darryl M. Bell onstage in a fireside chat that would later be broadcasted on my show, *The Culture Soup Podcast*®, which at that point made it to number six in Business News Apple Podcasts. I began my certified coach training two weeks later, and on May 1, 2019, I launched my private practice. What a ride it was.

Pressing Through Requires a Goal, a Plan, and Some Action

When working with leaders, through evidence-based exploration, we typically discover that one of the reasons leaders get stuck is because of their fear of something, whether it is fear of what others would say, fear of the unknown, or fear of something new or foreign. Fear is one of the most common ways that leaders stall in achieving their goal. Overcoming fear requires hope and information. Information minimizes the unknown, and hope enables goal achieving. After all, if you are hopeless, you likely have difficulty identifying a reason to move forward. Specific goals enable the brain to grasp onto details and visualize the way forward. I once heard a political science professor on a postelection 2024 panel say that Black people are hope addicts, especially in times when we face imminent danger to our civil rights or personhood. At this point, Vice President Harris had undergone what some called a decisive defeat in the election, in what many determined to be a fight for our democracy. In fact, the professor was dissuading Black people in particular from having "too much hope," as he ironically sat on this panel at a Black Church. There's scientific evidence that being "hope addicts" just might be one of Black America's superpowers, and the Black Church just might be one of our biggest hope dealers.

An article from the American Psychological Association calls hope "the antidote" to chaos and despair. The article outlines the importance of cultivating hope to sustain perseverance, particularly in difficult times, by reinforcing a positive vision of the future and the determination to achieve it. Without hope, there is no goal setting, and without the anticipation that drives that goal setting, there is no planning. With no plan, how do we then persevere? After the 2024 election, I heard so many people again and again tell others not to "raise their hopes" because they were afraid to be hopeful, but that fear isn't actually of hope itself. Our fear lies in the chance of disappointment that might be on the other side of it. Banking on disappointment is, in fact, planning to fail.

The APA article also declared that hope is a motivational force that enables humans to persevere, helping us to visualize a better future and identify concrete steps to achieve it. This has proven to build resilience in the individuals within the Black Church because the hope-filled worship, the songs, and sermons supply leaders with a positive outlook on their life and their work, even in the toughest situations. Neurologically speaking, hope activates the prefrontal cortex, where our executive functions occur. This is the area of the brain where goal setting, planning, and execution occur. In various conversations online after the election, I witnessed a common theme emerge: many people I interacted with believed that the concept of hope was a state of being, a feeling or emotion only. They proclaimed that hope without action was futile. Research in psychology reveals that hope that is activated in our brain isn't only about visualizing a better outcome; it's about putting plans into action. This neurological connection underscores how hope facilitates structured action and forward thinking. According to the APA, hope is not a passive emotion; it is an active practice of envisioning a positive future and mobilizing resources to make it happen.

Perseverance begins with a clear vision of success, enabled by hope, which empowers us to set clear goals. Hope also is powerful in other meaningful ways that separate leaders from incredible leaders:

Hope enables pathways thinking. Pathways thinking is a core element of hope, according to Hope Theory, and it helps us to identify multiple routes to overcome obstacles. Planning is a dynamic process and the core of perseverance.

Hope activates willpower. Hope initiates willpower because it is the energy that drives action toward goals. It also fuels the determination that powers perseverance.

Hope buffers the impact of stress. Hope serves as a psychological buffer against stress, strengthening coping abilities and resilience. Hopeful leaders are better equipped to handle adversity and inspire their teams to persist during challenging times.

Hope builds resilience. Hope escalates resilience, allowing leaders to traverse challenges and setbacks with resolve.

Hope reins in chaos. Hope helps leaders organize their thoughts and actions. Leaders who leverage hope are excellent at structured goal-setting practices and in persevering through uncertainty.

Hope jumpstarts problem-solving. Hopeful leaders are more adept at identifying solutions, viewing obstacles as opportunities for growth.

Hope enables visionary thinking. Hope enables leaders to envision success and good things to come in the future, inspiring their teams to work toward shared goals.

Having hope isn't actionless—science debunks that. Hope isn't hoping if it doesn't lead to an executable plan. Hope motivates organization. It inspires the brain's executive function to plot and take action. It is not hope if there is no action that follows. That's a wish. Hope is the accomplice that has helped Black people, often with the support of the social networks of the Black Church, overcome great obstacles over the course of history and persevere through adversity, and as the APA reminds us, amid chaos, hope provides a framework for order, turning aspirations into actionable steps.

That is perseverance.

THE LEADERSHIP LESSONS

Allow hope to fuel perseverance and goal achievement. Leaders who cultivate hope are more likely to set ambitious goals, persist through challenges, and inspire others to take action. Hope is not passive—it is the foundation for perseverance and success. Martin Seligman's research in positive psychology and Hope Theory describes hope as a "life-sustaining human strength" that consists of:

- **Goal Thinking:** setting clear, meaningful goals
- **Pathways Thinking:** identifying multiple strategies to reach those goals
- **Agency Thinking:** believing in one's ability to achieve success.

Hope activates the prefrontal cortex, which governs decision-making and problem-solving. Studies show that people with high levels of hope are more likely to develop concrete strategies to overcome obstacles.

Community Support Strengthens Leadership and Resilience. Successful leaders build and activate strong networks. Perseverance is sustained through community, collaboration, and strategic partnerships. Social cohesion—the shared sense of purpose within a community—has been shown to increase resilience and reduce stress. Studies from the NIH confirm that individuals with strong social support systems are more likely to persevere through adversity.

Visionary leadership requires strategic thinking and action. Perseverance is not just about enduring hardship—it is about taking decisive action. Leaders who anticipate challenges and craft strategies to navigate them are more likely to succeed. The APA defines perseverance as goal-directed behavior sustained over time, despite obstacles. Neurological studies show that strategic thinking activates the executive function of the brain, which enhances problem-solving and long-term planning.

Hope and anticipation drive motivation and mental resilience. Leaders who anticipate future success experience higher motivation, stronger resilience, and greater well-being. The ability to envision a positive future sustains perseverance. Dopamine, the "anticipation neurotransmitter," plays a crucial role in motivation and well-being. Research confirms that forward-looking expectancy has a more powerful effect on mood and resilience than recalling past successes.

Perseverance is strengthened by a clear plan of action. Leaders who turn hope into structured action are more likely to achieve their goals and sustain perseverance through challenges. The APA highlights that hope is not just a feeling—it is a structured practice. Studies show that people who set specific goals, develop pathways, and take action steps are more likely to persevere through difficult situations.

COACHING QUESTIONS

The last time you faced adversity, uncertainty, or a steep challenge, how did you respond?

How can you engage hope and anticipation to stoke determination and perseverance in the people you lead?

When was the last time you felt hopeless? If you were to face an equally adverse challenge, how might you approach it knowing what you now know about the power of perseverance?

6
COLLABORATION
Leadership in a Song

My uncle was on his deathbed recently, and my aunt called us over to have some final moments with him. It would take a couple of weeks before he'd actually pass on, so we were glad to have more than one time to share with him. The death of a loved one is tough, especially since it also means that besides mourning there's business to handle, and my aunt was on it. She was already planning the funeral on our first visit. She asked my mother and me into the living room while my father had some time with his brother, one of his older twin brothers whom he cherished.

There we were, sitting on the floral sofa, surrounded by golden chandelier scales and lamps on the coffee and end tables along with other beaded, opulent, and somewhat gaudy decor. It definitely reflected the style of the 1970s and '80s in any middle-class Black household. It was like we'd stepped back in time. My aunt pulled out a piece of paper, then turned and looked at me directly.

"You want to sing, right, Michelle?" she said.

Now, what's next, I didn't say out loud.

I haven't sung like that in years, I thought. What would I sing? Who would be my musician? Did I really want to make my uncle's funeral my comeback—with the side of my family looking on that had no clue I was a classically trained mezzo-soprano, former R&B cover band singer, and praise team member who'd sung backup for gospel and contemporary Christian artists, but had to put it all down, at least for a while, to become a professional speaker and author?

But I responded aloud, "Certainly!" because who says no to a grieving widow's face, let alone a Black church lady peering over her readers at you? What I didn't know was that my uncle would pass about two weeks later, the day before my daughter and I boarded a plane for Hawaii for spring break. The funeral was planned for the day after we returned on a red-eye.

This appeared to be my out, especially since they hadn't located a musician, so I graciously explained that I'd be in no shape to sing on that particular date. She seemed to understand, until the next day, when I had a drink with a tiny umbrella in hand on the beach—the text came from my mother.

"They moved your uncle's funeral a week out, so you can sing now. Your aunt found a musician. Let her know what you're going to sing."

Great. I'd been rebooked, and by my far-too-enthusiastic mother, who hadn't heard me sing in years. I have nicknamed her "Sarge." She wouldn't admit it, but she was pushing for it too. She said she couldn't say no to my aunt on my behalf, because, well, my aunt pretty much just *told* her that I would sing now without actually asking. And besides, again, she was a grieving widow. My mother, being a willful Black church lady herself, could have stood up to another like her, however, gracefully and seasoned with salt. So that explanation just didn't pass the smell test with me.

If this had been a twenty-year-old me, I would have been a bit anxious about things. Who *was* this random musician? What song would I sing? But after fifty-plus years in the Black Church and most of that time singing in the choir or leading from the platform for congregations as small as ten to fifteen people, to multiple services on the same Sunday, filled with thousands and thousands of people, and having access to a prolific canon of church songs, Old 100s, hymns, and praise and worship tunes both gospel and Christian contemporary *in my head*, I was reminded that I could compete and win in a game of Black Church Music Jeopardy with my eyes closed while singing the questions.

"I'll take Hymns of the Black Church for four hundred, Alex!"

"This song typically opened more formal Black Church services, and with no refrains or choruses, the lyrics proclaim, 'Stand up, stand up for Jesus!' my imaginary Trebek would read from his cue cards.

"What is hymn number 1 in the Baptist Standard Hymnal?!" I would answer after slamming that make-believe buzzer before anyone could even breathe. I can distinguish a Methodist hymn from a Presbyterian one, and I can even lead a COGIC battle cry if the Spirit moves. Russ Taff or Sandi Patty? Winans or Commissioned. Maverick City, Bethel Music, Hillsong, Planetshakers, Israel Houghton, Kirk Franklin, or Kari Jobe—I could not only sing along in the car or in the shower to them, but I could deliver many of their songs as a solo or lead a congregation in worship, directing the band or leading a mass choir of two hundred or more. No matter the size of the audience, I realized this superpower about the age of twelve, when my music minister asked me to lead a song with the adult choir, the Ollie Lee Scruggs Mass Choir, full of seasoned singers and saints. Thanks to appointments like that, and years and years under the tutelage of some of the Black Church's, nay, the country's or perhaps the world's, best music directors and artists, I knew how to stand and deliver in one of the "judgiest" arenas in music—the Black Church. I also realized that the musician would more than likely have those kinds of chops, being able to "catch me" no matter what key I began in.

Try me out on some Negro Spirituals? I've got you, thanks to the National Association of Negro Musicians (NANM), where I was an active member for years and sang under the most prolific clinicians on the planet. All of the clinicians and musicians were from the Black Church. How about an anthem or even a Requiem in Hebrew or Latin? I have you covered, and my *Messiah* score was always handy for a sing-along at Christmas no matter the church, white or Black. In fact, my father legendarily hid my Handel's *Messiah* long-playing record (LP) when I was four years old because I played the "Hallelujah Chorus" around the clock, every day of the week. He also allowed my mother to take the fall for that until recently; she outed him. I first heard the song at my church growing up, not in a concert hall. Yes, I had *Messiah* on wax as a child. I could sing all the parts before I ever had a vocal coach or joined a choir or chorus. Thanks to the Gospel Music Workshop of America (GMWA) and its members—again, all church musicians and artists—a Walter or Tremaine Hawkins song or an Andraé or Sandra Crouch tune was so easy to call up from memory faster than you could wave a church fan. In fact, I wasn't too surprised yet I was a little amused when one of my favorite soul singers struggled with the words to "Goin' Up Yonder." She had them taped to the back of a church fan during Aretha Franklin's funeral. She didn't grow up in the traditional Black Church that I write about. A quick internet search reveals that Chaka Khan grew up Catholic, and in my experience, the "higher" the church experience—the denser or more rigid the rituals—the less you were exposed to the rich traditions of what we can all agree is a bona fide Black Church service, or funeral service for that matter.

Dr. Henry Louis Gates Jr. makes the distinction of the denominations within the Black Church tradition clear. In his book *The Black Church: This Is Our Story, This Is Our Song*, Gates points out which Black churches have mainly been the originators and keepers of the Black Church experience. He cites seven historical Black denominations stemming from the Methodist, Baptist, and Pentecostal traditions: the African Methodist Episcopal Church (AME), the African Methodist Episcopal Zion Church (AME Zion), the National Baptist Convention (NBC), the National Baptist Convention, USA (NBCUSA), the Progressive National Baptist Convention (PNBC), the Christian Methodist Episcopal Church (CME), and the Church of God in Christ (COGIC).

Within this Black Church tradition, someone is always going to comment on how well the funeral home did with the body, as Jesse Jackson did from the pulpit during the Queen of Soul's funeral. Just as Tremaine Hawkins's version of "Goin' Up Yonder," "I'll Fly Away," or "When We All Get to Heaven" from the New Standard Baptist Hymnal are standard recessionals at funerals, so is commentary about how the body is presented at Black funerals. I've performed "Goin' Up Yonder" many times adjacent to many caskets. Black Twitter lit up like a bonfire at a Texas college pep rally when Chaka

Khan had the words to that song on the back of a church fan live on CNN. Most agreed that between that and Rev. Jackson's statement, the funeral included some of the Blackest moments ever simulcast on national television.

What was the leadership lesson in me being basically "voluntold" to sing at my uncle's funeral? There were three lessons in it: For one, I could relax. I didn't need rehearsals because I was overly prepared after years on years of singing both professionally and as an amateur in church. The second lesson wasn't so obvious. I learned grace, polish, and near perfection under fire. It was expected. While these were people of God looking on while you performed a song, you would indeed know if it didn't go well. While they didn't use the big hook or a tap-dancing Sandman from the Apollo Theatre, you may hear or feel rumblings after or get a good, yet gentle "talking to" by the music director or minister of music. The biggest lesson I learned while being in the music ministry in the Black Church was collaboration.

Collaboration Is Essential in the Music Ministry

When the time came for my uncle's funeral, I had neither reached back out to my aunt to tell her what I'd sing nor tried to connect with the musician. I had a couple of songs in mind, and based on the flow of the funeral, I'd choose before heading to the mic.

When the minister called my name, I walked to the organist, whispered, "'How Great Thou Art,' please. We'll do the first verse and the chorus twice. Follow me. Great to see you again." I recognized him from some church where I'd sung before. I was in good hands because unless you are in the deep country where the church only convenes once a month because the pastor is a circuit preacher, and the musician is ninety years old, somebody is going to play for you who knows all the music or can pick it up quickly.

He said, "You want to start?" I nodded.

I did.

He caught me.

We did that.

And it was as if we'd practiced ahead of time.

It isn't as if there aren't plenty of other places in the Black Church where we collaborate. There are. In fact, funerals are a great example. Sure, the funeral home plans the service with the family, but coordinating the service itself, the repast after and anything that happens throughout, falls on church members. Executives that I spoke with recall the many dinners on the ground, the many outreach and internal ministries, small groups, and the like that thrived on collaboration. But the music ministry is likely the one undeniable place where collaboration is taken to new levels and put on display so everyone can see the result. Yes, it can have its own brand of drama, but in Sunday morning service, even for those one or two hours of worship, the focus is on providing the one thing besides the preaching that keeps the congregation actively engaged in the service. The music is, no doubt, tone setting, and it is also the one "business unit" within the Black Church that is a true keeper and sustainer of the Black Church experience and culture.

"Today I'm sitting in the office in rural Indiana . . . and I turn on Hammond organ music. Today I feel like I'm sitting in a Black church," reflected Rev. Cokiesha Bailey Robinson, associate dean of mentoring and cross cultural engagement at Grace College in Evansville, Indiana. She is a preacher and a writer as well as the daughter of notable contributor to the art and science of expository preaching in the Black Church, the founder of Concord Church in Dallas, Rev. E. K. Bailey.

"I have so many positive memories from the sound of the Hammond organ," Robinson said. "When I think about the sounds of the Black Church, I think about the Hammond, the pipe organ, quartets and praise teams and gospel choirs. I think about youth ministry."

Rev. Robinson's first memory of leading in church was not of preaching or speaking. Long before she heard or heeded the call to preach (she then became the first and only Black dean at Grace College), at about the age of six, she dressed in her "Voices of Love" choir T-shirt and sang a solo with the children's choir.

Singer/songwriter David Frazier still remembers the first solo he sang at the Bible Way Church in Brooklyn, New York, at a very young age. It was a song called "I Made a Vow to the Lord."

"At five and six years old, I sang in the children's choir and was given a microphone to lead the song," said Frazier. "It starts early. And I think once any kind of talent or interest is recognized, it is somewhat encouraged. And then you, the individual, have your own personal application or personal drive to develop it."

It seems like a natural rite of passage for someone who would ultimately write the songs that church people sing inside and outside of its walls and hear on gospel radio, but the interesting thing is that singing in the church choir and even performing a solo is a common experience that these high-powered executives who grew up in the Black Church share. Wall Street powerhouse Carla Harris of Morgan Stanley was singing in both Baptist and Catholic churches by the age of thirteen, according to her official bio. She still sings today, after having hosted a solo gospel concert at Carnegie Hall in the year 2005 and recording her own albums and a single that serves as her "walkout" music when she mounts corporate and conference platforms to speak. Trudy Bourgeois, the retired equity strategist, and Adrion Porter, the professional speaker and mid-career expert, both recalled having experience in the music ministry; neither claim to be singers. Dominique "Dom" Jones, the talent and leadership consultant and expert who spent years at companies like AT&T, Southwest Airlines, and Varsity Brands, had to play, sing, and even preach on demand when his father told him to when he was barely eight years old.

Frazier said that corporate executives singing in the choir at very young ages isn't surprising to him because when most of these executives and he were growing up, all of them millennials, Gen Xers, or boomers, the church really only offered a handful of ways to lead: preaching and teaching, ushering and hospitality, and music, where you likely sang, but you also had the opportunity to play an instrument or direct. Back-office roles included ministry leadership and operations, and that was that.

Frazier pointed to the choir and music ministry as the primary spaces where individuals learn to collaborate, work as a team, and develop leadership qualities that are applied in other areas of life. However, in all these occasions when you could lead in church, but especially in the music ministry, church members had to learn to work together and, in this case, in harmony.

"It's about the blend," said renowned opera singer and businesswoman Denyce Graves, who wouldn't have discovered her talent for singing if she hadn't been told to sing in church, filling in for her brother, who was typically the lead in the little singing group her siblings formed. Her brother was under the weather, and instead of passing up the opportunity for the group to sing in church, her mother demanded she fill in and lead. The self-described "shy one" of her siblings told me that the choir forces you to really listen, to work with other people, and to understand that your voice is part of a larger sound.

"That's the power of the music ministry—it's a lesson in collaboration," Graves said. But first, she had to work together with her brother and sister while they were growing up as latchkey kids in Washington, DC. Before heading to work each evening on her second job, her single mother passed out assignments to work on in addition to the ones they brought home from school. After they finished their homework, they had a specific chore or duty. Mondays might be for sewing, so they would work to mend the holes in their socks or to dress up their dolls in their handmade designer creations. Wednesdays may be for cleaning, so that the house would be sparkling on their mother's return. Thursdays, however, were all about music. One day, their mother came home and they sang a song or two that they made up themselves, and she was so excited; she said that someone needed to hear them.

"So, my brother, sister, and I formed a little group called the Inspirational Children of God. We started singing at home and eventually in the church. It was our first taste of music ministry, learning to harmonize, blend our voices, and connect with the congregation."

Had her brother not been under the weather that Sunday, the world may not have met and claimed Graves as "The World's Favorite Carmen." She has graced world stages from the Metropolitan Opera to the Royal Opera House in London to the Vienna State Opera and has become the leading mezzo-soprano that so many know and love today. Her powerful voice, stage presence, and dedication to her craft have made Denyce Graves a highly respected figure in the world of opera, and it all started at the Faith Church of God and Son, now known as the Faith Bible Church in Washington, DC.

Black Church Music Teaches Emotional Intelligence

When Graves speaks of the way singing together in the Black Church is collaboration in action, with its chord progressions and distinct triads, she is talking about the blending of voices and the listening that's necessary to produce a collective, rich sound. It sparks a great analogy: that listening and blending is to a singer in church as tapping into emotional intelligence is to a leader in a business environment. The self-awareness a leader must have is crucial when working together with anyone, and reading the room amounts to feeling what is happening around you in a space. This is active listening with your eyes and ears. You also need to feel the Spirit, channeling it through yourself to minister to those in the sanctuary, and a singer must feel that Spirit within the space in order to pivot and deliver what the congregation needs in the moment. If you are singing and leading on the platform, you're not only doing all of that, but you may also be cuing the band and bringing in the singers behind you. Backup singers need to know the music, but they also need to know, watch, listen to, and respond to the lead singer. Choir members must keep an eye on the director, but must not forget to minister to the congregation. There is a lot of feeling going on, and the music goes where it wants to go, taking all that into consideration.

The choir and music ministry is a microcosm of the systems

within the larger Black Church experience because, arguably, it is its own business school. Singing in the choir and even playing in the band or orchestra teaches even more leadership lessons:

Community building: Singing in a choir fosters a deep sense of unity and belonging. Members build lasting friendships, strengthening their bonds with one another and the larger congregation.

Trust and support: Choir members learn to trust one another, collaborating toward shared goals.

Humility and willingness to learn: In the choir, everyone is on a journey of growth, realizing that no single person holds all the expertise.

Listening: Choir members develop the skill to harmonize with others, adjusting their tune rather than overpowering.

Valuing each member: Every voice in the choir is valuable, and the group feels the impact when even one member is absent.

Relationship building: The collaboration is rooted in strong relationships and creates a solid, appealing dynamic, sound, and performance.

Diversity: A mix of people with different talents, talent levels, and voice parts brings diversity, and the unique ideas these people contribute lead to true inclusion.

Praise from the Choir Stand Is About Brain Power

New neural pathways are blazed in the brain the minute you learn that you need to be ready at a moment's notice, and once that behavior is repeated, you learn to expect it, and eventually, you just do it. This is the core concept within neuroplasticity. Our brains are malleable, and even more so as children. Enough of this repeated action and you've learned a new behavior, reenforced by positive feedback and rewards, activating the progress loop; you will come back for more.

Along with the positive feedback, the act of singing also activates the brain's reward system. This releases endorphins, dopamine, and serotonin, according to a study released nearly a decade ago. These hormones are associated with feelings of pleasure, trust, bonding, and serenity. Singing also increases activity in the medial prefrontal cortex, which is connected to the limbic system. That study concludes that there is a positive effect on one's physical health and well-being when people sing together. Our heartbeats also sync.

Recall that the connections that are formed within community trigger oxytocin in the brain, which neuroscience calls the "bonding" or "love" hormone. The act of singing worship songs together fosters a deep sense of unity and collaboration. It's a choir or praise team member's opportunity to connect beyond words and to work together in rhythm, which fosters a sense of cooperation. This isn't something that began in the Black Church; it has roots in the cotton fields during pre–Civil War times when enslaved people would sing together to elevate themselves beyond the hard work and toil and shift their minds, hearts, and mental focus to something bigger than themselves—the anticipation of Canaan's Land. Even if they knew they wouldn't get there one day, they knew that perhaps their children would. Because the idea of Canaan was as much about freedom from bondage as it was about heaven's pearly gates, the songs and worship of Black people are just plain different from what you might hear in another church of a different culture. Black culture is a culture founded in the midst of suffering. It's why the songs and worship from the Black Church "hit different," as the younger generations would say. Frederick Douglass commented on the songs of slavery, saying that the deep, soul-stirring singing he grew up hearing "was a testimony against slavery, and a prayer to God for deliverance from chains. . . . To those songs I trace my first glimmering conceptions of the dehumanizing character of slavery."

Rev. Robinson said that suffering and the yearning for freedom from it are embedded in church music. "A Black church doesn't forget suffering. A Black church doesn't forget the sounds of a Black church," she said.

Layer onto the culture and history of Black worship and singing, the biology of it, that it literally can rewire the brain, and the collision of culture and science becomes a potent spiritual cocktail unique to the Black Church experience. Someone might just "shout," "get happy," "go in," and that's exactly what the choir is there to help facilitate—the ushering in and the movement of the Spirit throughout the worship experience in order that everyone just might get a glimpse of what heaven is like. No wonder the Black Church choir, which I've described as a locomotive with its power and driving rhythms and the soul that soul music borrows from, no matter the size, can move through the church service in the most cohesive way to usher in, well, glory, whether you were expecting it, wanted it to, or not.

CALL AND RESPONSE

Teamwork Makes the Dream Work

Choir members in the Black Church learn to work with people they may not necessarily befriend outside the choir stand. This leads to the kind of teamwork that yields peak performance, something leaders strive for in the workplace. It's where people move in lockstep; they can anticipate a teammate's move and can step up with tools and resources that address a need before the other even realizes they had one. It's the blind trust that choir members develop in their director because he or she just may take that song anywhere. In the case of gospel music, the song is definitely not confined to sheet music. You may repeat and vamp until the congregation is on its feet. You may keep singing when the director cues the musicians to stop. The lead soloist may slow things down or speed things up. You have to be ready. The traditional Black gospel choir understands the power of the pivot and can anticipate what each person beside them or even in other sections may or may not do in the moment. Even in the singing of an anthem, where the singers adhere to the written music, the ability to go from gutbucket handclapping and foot-stomping music to high-church choral music is something that is unique to the Black Church choir. It's the kind of agility for which any business leader yearns from their teams and organizations.

Singing in choirs, and by extension playing instruments to accompany them, teaches individuals the importance of working together toward one goal. Black Church choir members develop not only the ability to harmonize musically, but also teamwork, decision-making, and community-building skills. It always felt so good after the choir at my home church finished an A or B selection. Not only could we witness the impact on the congregation, we felt it too. It wasn't simply a sense of accomplishment, but it was also a feeling that we needed each other to complete something that we couldn't have done by ourselves. Over the years, I've enjoyed singing with the huge gospel choirs of the 1980s and '90s, the small ensembles and praise teams that became popular in the early 2000s, and I've even enjoyed singing background vocals for gospel artists.

When the Choir Is Made of Leaders, the Teamwork Is Top Tier

Creating the very first all-journalist choir for the National Association of Black Journalists (NABJ) has been one of my favorite undertakings because it was part event coordination, part gospel music workshop, and part startup. I had to flex every leadership skill I had at the time. The NABJ Coast-to-Coast choir appeared for the first time at the NABJ Convention hosted in Dallas in 2003. Because the local chapter was hosting, it was on us to provide and execute programming ideas that would engage the conventioneers and create positive buzz about our chapter and our city. One of the most popular events at the convention is the gospel brunch on Sunday as the convention closes for the week. Typically, the organization secures a gospel artist to perform at the brunch. Because I knew that a number of journalists sang in their local church choirs, I thought it would be a good idea to have a choir made up of NABJ members open for that year's guest, three-time Grammy Award–winning gospel artist Donnie McClurkin.

Recruiting the members was fairly simple, because when they

received their invitations, many responded enthusiastically. Rehearsing these singing journalists would be challenging though, because as the name of the choir implied, they were located all over the United States and would only be together for a few days during the convention when it convened in Dallas over a long weekend near the beginning of August. So, the project structure seemed obvious to me. I would recruit a minister of music from a local church whom I knew from the Gospel Music Workshop of America to volunteer to "workshop" these communicators each day between convention programming and evening events, and on Sunday we'd take the stage. Every bit of the responsibility fell on me: coordinating the music selections; allocating what little budget we had for T-shirts; securing the rentals like risers, a top-of-the-line Hammond organ (because you really aren't having Black Church without one), and drums; finding an honorarium for the clinician; developing a logo and branding; scheduling rehearsals; and essentially running the operations for this new project and ensuring that the choir sounded good in time for Sunday's brunch. The journalists who showed up also included newspaper reporters, television news talent, editors, media executives, and even public relations people. I recall that we even landed a Pulitzer Prize winner from the *Wall Street Journal* for the tenor section. They all knew their voice parts—soprano, alto, tenor, bass-baritone—and they fell in line accordingly because they knew exactly what to do. They brought rich experiences with them from growing up in the Black Church. After the first rehearsal, which went a little long because several of us caught the spirit and didn't want to close out, that choir congealed. We were one body, with one mission: to bring a lot more church and a little more of the Holy Ghost to the gospel brunch. Our first director was Charles

Mitchell, who was at the time music minister at the Mt. Pisgah Baptist Church in Dallas. He selected "The Presence of the Lord Is Here," by Kurt Carr, and he executed my vision like the professional he was. Each choir member began in their seats in the audience, and as Mitchell started the song on the organ and sang lead, the song picked up pace, and journalists from all over the room and across the country ran to the stage in a sort of role call—East Coast, West Coast, Midwest, and Deep South. Before long, all choir members were in their places on the risers singing at the top of our lungs, rocking, swaying, and clapping in harmony.

It's safe to say that the convention floor was in pure pandemonium, because conventioneers were surprised to see their colleagues jump up from their seats and sprint to the stage. About thirty of us had managed to do exactly what the song said—we had ushered in the presence of the Lord, and it was euphoric. On top of that, the choir sounded like they'd been together for years, not simply days. I was, of course, on the risers singing soprano, but I got pulled. Donnie McClurkin was asking, "Whose choir is that?" He wanted to know... and he wanted to join us. Before long... he was onstage with us—and together, we truly had *church*.

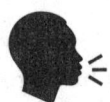

THE LEADERSHIP LESSONS

Agility and trust build high-performing teams. Successful leaders cultivate trust and adaptability within teams, allowing them to pivot seamlessly when circumstances change. Like a choir following a director's lead in real time, agile leaders know when to adjust, delegate, and step in where necessary. Research in neuroscience suggests that trust and cooperation are linked to oxytocin, the "bonding hormone," which fosters stronger group cohesion and enhances team performance. Additionally, neuroplasticity allows individuals to develop agility in decision-making through repeated exposure to dynamic team environments.

Collaboration creates stronger, more cohesive teams. High-performing teams understand the power of collaboration. Choirs exemplify this as members blend voices and harmonize, recognizing that no single person carries the performance alone. Leaders should cultivate this same interdependence in their teams. Studies indicate that strong collaboration improves problem-solving and innovation, as collective intelligence is greater than individual contributions. Additionally, social neuroscience reveals that shared goals and group participation activate neural pathways associated with motivation and engagement.

Emotional intelligence strengthens leadership presence. Leaders who develop their emotional quotient (EQ) are better equipped to manage teams, foster engagement, and navigate workplace challenges. Much like choir members who must attune to the emotions of the congregation, leaders must be able to "read the room" and adjust accordingly. Research shows that emotional intelligence correlates with stronger leadership effectiveness. The anterior insular cortex is activated when individuals engage in empathy, allowing leaders to sense team morale and respond appropriately.

Cultural awareness and inclusion foster innovation. Inclusive leadership requires an awareness of diverse perspectives, ensuring all voices are valued. The Black Church music tradition, rooted in historical struggle and resilience, exemplifies how diverse cultural elements create innovation and transformation. Research from social neuroscience highlights that diversity in thought and background leads to higher levels of creativity and innovation. Psychological safety, where individuals feel included and valued, has been shown to boost engagement and productivity.

Peak performance requires a strong support system. Elite teams and leaders don't succeed alone; they thrive within well-structured systems. Choirs exemplify this by relying on directors, musicians, and vocalists working in sync. Leaders who build supportive environments empower their teams to achieve at the highest levels. Neuroscience research shows that peak performance is linked to social support and positive reinforcement. The brain's reward system, activated through group singing, releases endorphins, dopamine, and serotonin, fostering trust and motivation.

COACHING QUESTIONS

What leadership lessons can you take from Black Church choirs and music ministries to apply to and improve on your work and your business in corporate America?

CALL AND RESPONSE

Now that your team must bond in order to perform at its peak, what will you do to foster team building and community building within your organization?

What can a Black Church choir teach us about people who have differences working together for a common goal, and how can you apply that to your leadership journey?

7
ACCOUNTABILITY
Keeping It Righteous

I'm not sure how I would respond if my doorbell rang on a Saturday morning and I answered it and found a nine-year-old girl asking if my daughter could board a bus to go to Sunday School. It's even harder to imagine that I'd say yes, but that is what many adults did in the DC area when a nine-year-old Denyce Graves made the rounds for her church.

"On Saturdays, I would go and knock on people's doors that had kids and ask them if they wanted their kids to come to Sunday School, and then sign those kids up for Sunday School," Graves said. "And then I would have to go pick them up on the church bus. Pick them up for Sunday School, take them to church to Sunday School and then get them back. And I had to be responsible to make sure we had Susie Q. I would sing songs on the bus to keep the kids entertained on the bus ride from the house to Sunday School."

Graves sang one of the call-and-response tunes that she sang with the children on the bus: "You Can't Get to Heaven on Roller Skates."

"I was the head of the bus ministry," she said.

Graves was learning accountability at a tender young age and didn't quite realize it yet. She simply knew she had a job to do, and she did it. Her duties entailed not only convincing the parents to release their children into her care, at least for the bus ride, but also keeping account of those children and getting them safely back home.

In it there were lessons in responsibility to others, building trust through communication, and commitment to service. Learning these leadership skills at such a young age does something to you, according to Graves and other business leaders. When I asked them why they were so driven, all replied that they were motivated from within to do the job to the best of their abilities.

Michael Hyter, CEO of the Executive Leadership Council, says that he was only seven years old when he first learned accountability. One of the ministers at the Ebenezer AME Church in Detroit assigned him to a special role in the youth-led service, a service that happened every fifth Sunday, on average four times a year. He called Ebenezer an extension of his home life. He was asked to read the scripture and introduce the preacher for the day. He recalls being extremely nervous, yet well-prepared, as his feet dangled because they didn't even reach the floor. His parents worked with him, drilling him so that he didn't miss a word when it was time to finally mount the block the church staff created for little people, so that they could reach the microphone and speak to approximately three hundred people in the pews.

"I credit preparation. It was a thing, and I was nervous about it," Hyter said. "But I had parents who encouraged me and were excited about it. We practiced and worked through it, and this is what you do at home. They took the time and then they reassured me I'd be okay."

Michael said that he learned responsibility, commitment, preparation, and leadership all at once, and he was affirmed when he actually pulled off the assignment and received adulation from the congregation and the church leadership.

"There was a lot of pride and a lot of great joy from people I didn't even know, like older people. I heard one elderly lady say, 'He's going to be a speaker someday,'" he said. "That affirmation was part of the dessert of being on the other side of it. I was just so happy that it was done, that it was over, because it was more than just the scripture."

When I asked him where he thought the accountability came from, he said that it mostly came from the inside. He acknowledged the role his parents and pastor played, but he said that although his knees were knocking when he was asked to do the task, he knew the gravity of it, and that it was something he just had to do. He explained that the same sense of self-motivated accountability drives him in business today.

He's not alone. Retired, history-making CEO of the NBA's Dallas Mavericks and former AT&T senior executive Cynthia Marshall delivered her first sermon at fifteen at the New Bethel Apostolic Holy Church. "Cynt," as we called her, is my former colleague from the telecom giant. She told me that it was a rite of passage in the Pentecostal church for many teens to preach because when it was youth night, they took over all the responsibilities in the order of worship, which is very typical in the Black Church. Her mother coached her through the preaching format, urging her to study and prepare for it.

"My mother would help with the outline. I was a smart kid, so I always liked to write," she said. "She just talked to us about the outline. You've got to have a subject, and she also taught us that you want it to be relevant. Always be in touch with what's going on in the environment . . . If we knew something was going on with our colleagues and all that, there was a scripture for everything."

There was no doubt in her mind that she needed to turn down weekend fun if it was the night she was to preach.

"I was accountable for what I had to get done. And it wasn't like somebody making me do it. I just knew it," Marshall said. "If a revival came to town, nobody had to tell us, 'Oh, you're going to service on Tuesday night.' We just knew we were going; we wanted to go. It was just a part of what we did. That accountability, that discipline, that focus—it all ended up making me who I am right now. How I approach life, how I approach work—it all goes together."

What Marshall described so passionately is what positive psychology calls intrinsic motivation. It's the drive that comes from deep within because whatever the thing is that gets you moving is aligned with your values. For Cynt and other executives like her, those values were and still are faith and purpose.

"That's what actually motivates me—I have this internal sense of knowing what I am supposed to do and that I have to do it," she said. "I don't shirk my responsibilities. I don't think, 'Okay, well, somebody could do that next week,' or 'It's okay to be late on that.' No, somebody is counting on that. And nobody needs to tell me that. I am motivated by a sense of duty, a sense of ownership. I'm accountable for what I am supposed to get done."

And does she ever still do that today. When people come into contact with her, they comment on her authenticity first, and they assume that is what makes Cynt the incredible leader that she is. They are not wrong; however, when you dig a little deeper, it really is her commitment to accountability that drives that authenticity and any other leadership trait she demonstrates. It's an ongoing theme throughout her life, and this is what transforms the organizations she leads. When Cynt became CEO of the Dallas Mavericks in 2018, she inherited an organization in crisis following a workplace misconduct scandal. She immediately launched a one-hundred-day plan focused on cultural transformation that emphasized, what else, *accountability*, first and foremost, *then* diversity and inclusion. She is well known for her work in the space, but rarely do people say that she is actually a master at accountability. Marshall overhauled HR policies, implemented zero-tolerance harassment standards, and ensured women and people of color were represented at all levels of leadership. Under her guidance, the Mavericks became a model for workplace equity in professional sports, earning national recognition for their commitment to transparency and inclusivity. Her turnaround not only restored trust within the organization but also redefined leadership standards in the NBA. By the way, she never stopped preaching either. Certainly, if you've heard any of her leadership speeches, you've been inspired, but to be clear, some days when Cynt stands up before a group of people, whether at a church or church conference, she "takes a text."

The Most Powerful Accountability Comes from the Inside

A great deal of research in positive psychology is dedicated to motivation, most specifically two kinds: extrinsic motivation, which adds pressure from the outside, and intrinsic motivation, which presses from within. While both are effective, the intrinsic kind is the most powerful because it derives from an alignment with our values, according to the popular accountability app GoalsWon. By the time young future executives are old enough to have observed modeled behavior, often through siblings or parents who are involved in church, they are able to connect the dots between their faith, a deeply held value that they ultimately adopted on their own, and the importance of the task or assignment to the bigger picture—whether it is how their task fit into the larger worship experience or the implication of building God's kingdom. For young people, this is an incredible responsibility to accept.

From a neuroscience perspective, this activates the reward center in the brain, where neurons fire off the dopamine hormone, which makes us feel really good about what we've done. It's the sense of accomplishment; when you hear amens from the congregation, that's even further affirmation, which kicks off a progress loop in the brain. For most executives, the progress loop they associate with the thrill of delivering while being held accountable never really ends.

It comes down to what psychologists Richard Ryan and Edward Deci call the self-determination theory, or the 4 C's of intrinsic motivation: challenge, curiosity, control, and context. It's human nature to be drawn into tasks or assignments that seem just beyond our reach, so when Black church leaders appoint youngsters to step into roles normally reserved for adults, the young person is given a welcome challenge. This kind of challenge also triggers our internal drive for personal growth. Curiosity fuels the desire for even further development, and these young churchgoers are not set off on training wheels but afforded the free rein of a pulpit, or in my case a solo microphone with the entire adult mass choir backing me up, or in the case of opera diva Denyce Graves an entire bus ministry. Young people are motivated to not only do the job but do the job to the best of their ability. Providing these children with context, that the job they've taken on has a major impact on the broader ministry or even at the macrolevel, the Kingdom, gives them the final aspect of the 4 C's.

Personal accountability is simply holding oneself responsible. In addition to increased motivation to achieve one's goals, according to positive psychology, holding oneself responsible can also lead to positive outcomes, including helping us to stay focused and achieve goals. It can boost our self-esteem and encourage personal growth, and self-awareness promotes stronger relationships. Personal accountability fosters a high degree of self-reflection that enables us to assess what adjustments we need to make personally in order to get a job done. In short, accountability means progress. If perseverance puts feet on resilience, accountability is the fuel that powers perseverance because it increases confidence and feelings of competency while helping us to weather setbacks, increasing resilience.

Sometimes Personal Accountability Comes to Light Through Others

Rev. Cokiesha Bailey Robinson, associate dean of mentoring and cross cultural engagement at Grace College, an author, and an ordained minister first encountered individual accountability in the church during her formative years, particularly as she navigated her calling to ministry. She reflected on how the Black Church played a crucial role in her growth, stating that it was a space where people were encouraged to "become in real time." Being nurtured within a supportive faith community helped her develop confidence and accountability for her own spiritual and leadership journey.

For context, Rev. Robinson grew up the daughter of prominent Dallas pastor Rev. E. K. Bailey, founder of the Concord Church, during a time when women preachers were generally frowned on, but gender never became an issue until she went away to college and was nearing graduation. While she grew up as a "P.K." or preacher's kid, Cokeisha was most often spotted in the children's choir; for her, leading most often meant performing an occasional solo.

However, the most pivotal moments in her personal accountability journey came as a young woman at Fisk University. She told me that she began having dreams about preaching, which initially left her feeling fear and resistance. She had no personal desire to preach. At that time, she struggled with reconciling her personal desires to be a journalist with what she believed God was calling her to do.

"I didn't grow up in a context where there were many women preachers; it felt weird to have a call," she said. "I thought if God wanted me to be that, wouldn't I have had female models? But He was saying, 'Be what you don't see.'"

A defining moment of accountability occurred on her graduation day from Fisk when Dr. Christina Archibald, the esteemed dean of chapel at Fisk, told Cokiesha's sister, "Nothing that she wants to do in life will pan out until she acknowledges that God has called her to do it." Archibald's assertion stopped Cokiesha in her tracks.

"Now I know at my age, so much makes sense in the rearview mirror, but as a young person with hopes and dreams, and that's not a part of it, you don't know how to reconcile what you haven't become when God shows you that's what you'll be."

From that moment on, she recognized that accountability wasn't just about external validation but about her own willingness to accept responsibility for her gifts, leadership, and faith journey.

Her story underscores how personal accountability in the church is both a communal and an individual process—rooted in mentorship, faith, and the courage to step into one's purpose. She offered some advice to any leaders about accepting and adhering to one's accountability—understandings that she has embraced along the way as a reluctant trailblazer:

Know and honor boundaries: Understanding one's limits and not overcommitting is crucial. She has exercised boundary setting when, for instance, someone asked her to be their mentor. Instead of answering immediately, pause to reflect to see if that is something you have the capacity for before overpromising. Do not say yes to something your schedule won't allow. She framed good leadership as knowing one's capacity and setting boundaries accordingly.

Self-reflection and growth: Evaluating progress is a necessity, as is acknowledging both successes and failures. She stated, "A good leader can evaluate his or her challenges," and mentioned celebrating wins while also critiquing areas that need improvement.

Maintaining hope and perseverance: She stressed that a good leader never "calls the benediction on hope," meaning they must remain hopeful and resilient despite challenges, a crucial mindset she deems core to personal accountability. She suggests that individuals should not only strive forward but also recognize that setbacks and perseverance are part of growth.

Learning to pivot and adapt: Also core to accountability, good leaders must remain flexible, acknowledging that success often comes from the ability to adjust and move forward. She noted that learning is cyclical, requiring people to reassess and refine their actions continuously.

Prioritizing mental health and self-care: Noting the generational shift in acknowledging mental health, leaders should embrace taking vacations, prioritizing therapy and self-care. She emphasized that resilience should not come at the cost of personal well-being.

Authenticity and embracing one's calling: She reflected on her own journey of accepting her calling, even when it was unexpected or different from her original plans. She talked about the fear and resistance she initially had, questioning how she could be something she didn't see modeled. Ultimately, she recognized the importance of stepping into her purpose despite personal doubts, holding herself accountable to the call.

Accountability to Others Abounds in the Black Church

The Black Church, as any other church, has been criticized for not holding its own leadership accountable, namely, some of the pastors. Like with any organization of faith or otherwise, the Black Church has had its fair share of criticism and scandals, but, on the whole, these executive leaders had positive interactions and experiences with their church leadership, which shows that when leadership accountability works the way it should, the positive fruits are plentiful.

No one likely can relate better to the criticism regarding church leadership accountability than a good Catholic. At least two of the executives I spoke with were christened Catholic, but somehow they found themselves in a Baptist church, a denomination focused on people, communal and individual responsibility, and dedication to learning the Word for oneself. Recall that retired Fortune 500 executive, author, and equity consultant Trudy Bourgeois attended Catholic services with her mother, and some Sundays she walked with her grandmother, who was all dressed up in an oversized hat and matching suit, down the street to the Baptist church where she sang in the children's choir.

A thirteen-year-old Carla Harris, who is now a notable executive in the financial world, was also born into Catholicism, but somehow she found herself singing solos in the youth choir at a Black Baptist Church that wasn't too far away from her home. Growing up in Jacksonville, Florida, Harris played with neighborhood friends on the sidewalks in her free time. One of their favorite things to do was sing together. Her friends, all Baptist, would teach her the gospel songs, and she would harmonize with them. At one point, one of her friends encouraged her to not only come to their church but to also ease into the choir stand and be a part of the youth choir. Harris didn't hesitate.

"I would literally, from eighth grade to twelfth grade, go to mass and then have my mama drop me off at the Baptist church; and I would sing there," Harris said. "And that's how I learned to sing gospel music."

It didn't matter that she was a dedicated member of the St. Pius V Catholic Church. She was more than happy to sing on Sunday morning at the St. Paul Missionary Baptist Church and also attend the rehearsals during the week. This went on for five years, until one day when Harris was a senior in high school, the pastor pulled her over to the side.

"He called me into his office," she said. "And, of course, I was nervous that this was going to be it. And he said, 'You know, Ms. Harris, it's come to my attention that you're singing in my choir and you're not a member of my church.' And I said, 'No, Reverend Taylor, I am not.' And he said, 'Well, you know, you need to be a member of the church in order to be a member of the choir. Are you intending to become a member of our church?' And I said, 'No, Reverend Taylor, I am not. I am Catholic. I've been Catholic since I was three months old. I don't have any interest in changing my affiliation.'

"He said, 'So what am I supposed to tell people when they ask me why you're singing in my choir?' I said, 'Boy, I don't know, Reverend Taylor.'

"So he paused. He looked down, and then he said, 'Well, I'll just tell them that you're enjoying Jesus any way you can.'"

That one move set off a career for Harris, but not the financial one. Harris learned to sing gospel so well that she now hosts sold-out, one-woman gospel concerts at Carnegie Hall, the Apollo Theatre in Harlem, and other notable venues. Harris also records. However, those lessons in accountability, teamwork, and servant leadership, as well as all the scriptures that she memorized, helped her to earn and hold on to her positions in banking; she's now one of the top financial officers at Morgan Stanley.

"You had to show up to rehearsals if you were expected to sing. That was a level of accountability. And you were accountable for knowing your music. You couldn't get up there and sing if you didn't know the music," Harris said. "Now, presumably, you would learn the music at rehearsal. But even if you only got introduced to the music at rehearsal, it was your job to kind of work on it between the time that you learned it or was introduced to it for the first time and the time you actually had to perform. That was accountability."

While she was in that Baptist youth choir, she also learned how to be a follower, another form of leadership, she says, that keeps one accountable. She says to be a great leader, you shouldn't always clamor to be out front. Being a good follower shows that you can submit to others who lead.

"Being a good follower is obviously somebody who's focused on what the leadership is saying, who the leadership is, how the leadership is engaging," she said. "It gives you a certain level of relationship, if you will, with a leader if you are a good follower. It also trains you to be a good listener. And so being somebody who was in that church, in that choir, that was not supposed to be there . . . who was definitely perpetrating because I wasn't a member of the church. So I would argue that made me a particularly good follower because I wanted to comport myself in a certain way where nobody would say, 'Hey, you! What are you doing in here anyway?'"

Creating a culture that encourages leadership accountability accomplishes many things that are important in workplace cultures.

Enhances employee performance and engagement. Accountability is crucial for improving performance and building a positive culture.

Helps to establish trust and respect. Employees hold accountable leaders to high standards, leading to increased engagement and retention.

Fosters a culture of growth. Accountability can enhance company culture by promoting growth and helping employees reach their full potential.

Clarifies roles and responsibilities. Accountability involves understanding individual roles and performance goals, including standards for measuring success.

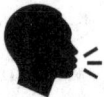

THE LEADERSHIP LESSONS

Accountability starts with owning responsibility. True accountability begins when individuals internalize their responsibilities rather than waiting for external pressure. In leadership, the best performers don't wait to be reminded—they take ownership. Effective leaders see tasks through and ensure their teams do the same.

Preparation demonstrates accountability. Excellence comes from preparation, which is a leader's responsibility to themselves and those they serve. Leaders who prepare diligently earn trust and respect. Those who cut corners or come unprepared risk damaging their credibility.

Internal motivation is the strongest accountability. The most effective leaders are driven by an internal sense of duty, not just external rewards or consequences. Leaders should cultivate intrinsic motivation by aligning work with their values. Accountability feels less like a burden when it is tied to purpose.

Leadership accountability includes service to others. A leader is responsible for those they guide, making servant leadership a core component of accountability. Accountability in leadership means ensuring that organizations are transparent, fair, and committed to ethical standards.

Being a good follower is a leadership skill. Leadership is not always about being out front; sometimes, accountability means knowing how to follow and support others. In business, great leaders are also great team players. They support initiatives, uplift colleagues, and understand when to lead versus when to follow.

Mentorship and guidance foster accountability. Sometimes, others hold us accountable before we even recognize our calling. Good leaders recognize when others need a push to step into their purpose and hold them accountable to their potential.

Holding organizations accountable builds trust. Leaders must ensure accountability extends beyond individuals to the culture of an organization. Leaders who demand accountability at all levels cultivate trust, loyalty, and long-term success in their organizations.

COACHING QUESTIONS

How do you currently hold yourself accountable in your leadership role, and where might you need to strengthen that accountability?

Think of a time when you had to balance personal responsibility with the needs of a team or organization. How did you navigate that challenge, and what did you learn from the experience?

Who are the mentors, colleagues, or team members who help keep you accountable? How can you cultivate a culture of shared accountability within your organization?

Reflecting on the intrinsic motivation that drives you, how can you better align your personal values with the way you lead and hold yourself accountable?

8

SOCIAL JUSTICE

A Legacy of Overcoming

I experienced a pivotal moment in my churchgoing life during the 2024 election season when I noticed that something was missing from the worship service at the ten-thousand-member nondenominational church that I'd been attending for a couple years. It hadn't been obvious until that point because we were not in an election season, and we were not faced with an immediate and present threat to the personhood and civil rights of Black people. That threat emerged in the form of the Republican presidential nominee who'd been fairly brash in his conversations about Black people and other marginalized groups. Despite seeing Vice President Kamala Harris address congregations from the pulpits of several Black churches toward the end of her campaign and also knowing that in this moment in time our livelihoods, along with many others, were at stake because of the proposed policies of her opponent, I wasn't feeling what I thought I should feel when I attended my church. The pastor had gone to great lengths to underscore to the congregation that while everyone was welcome, this was indeed a Black Church. It also serves other cultures—including that of white evangelicals fleeing Christian nationalism for something that was a lot more exciting and made them feel more at home with no real political discourse. To his credit, the pastor of the church went to some lengths to keep many of the traditions going, especially through his writings, which often become sermon series or Bible studies; the church has a choir that also sings everything from Walter Hawkins to Kirk Franklin songs, and even some spirituals from time to time. However, the liberation theology that I had grown up with at the Good Street Baptist Church, where my pastor had welcomed Dr. Martin Luther King Jr. many years before I was born, was missing.

That particular morning, when it dawned on me that social justice was missing from the mix at my church, I climbed the stairs to wake my daughter instead of FaceTiming her because this Sunday morning would be a little different. For two years we had attended this nondenominational church in person. I had made the move from a smaller, yet still mega-by-any-standards church down the street where I'd been a member for about seventeen years previously. I told her that this morning I didn't feel like putting in the struggle to get to that massive sanctuary. At twelve, she more than understood the tedious ritual: the parking blocks away only to take a shuttle in, and only if we made a certain window were we able to obtain my preferred seats on the main floor just rows from the platform. A moment too late, and we were relegated to the balcony, where it seemed so removed that the live stream feels more intimate, and if that happened, it felt like all that struggle to park and walk and shuttle was wasted. To be clear, my challenge wasn't simply about the struggle to park and get all my ten thousand steps in for the day on the way to the sanctuary; it was about the *Strug-*

gle. Instead of making that sojourn, we would venture back to my previous church where my parents and sister still attended an earlier service. We knew that we could be a few minutes late and still get a nice parking spot up close, take only a few steps to the front door, find a seat on the floor, but most important, we would hear a word and a song that was meaningful to my entire being. Maverick City Music or Hillsong praise and worship tunes just wouldn't do it for me on this particular morning. I needed the Black Church to do for me what only the Black Church can do for my Black soul in such a time as we found ourselves—only a little over a week away from the election. On that particular Sunday the reality sank in that the country might just reject yet another overqualified Black woman in favor of a mediocre white man, a candidate convicted of felonies, a failed presidential track record, and someone who talked about "black jobs" and maligned Vice President Harris in every stereotypical and misogynistic way possible.

I needed the Black Church to pour back into me what society snatches away with every news cycle, tense political discussion with friends who seem to be voting against their own interests, and a social media news stream that is literally "too much" on a daily basis. The Black Church has this unique ability to restore, with the power of a good word and great music grounded in deep cultural traditions like the call and response, its ability to organize and mobilize, and its historical focus on overcoming the greatest odds against its people.

Hearing only about the Christian me isn't enough for this champion of moving more women and especially Black women to the C-Suite, this great-granddaughter of a woman who was born on a plantation, with my daughter, who is only one more generation removed from that and whose Blackness and womanhood were both threatened by the outcome of the election ten days in the future. Receiving that solid dose of social justice and liberation theology was something I knew I couldn't quite receive from my church at the time. They would typically only point you to a table after worship to ensure that you're registered to vote. You're guaranteed not to hear a peep about how your Black body may be in jeopardy. We were encouraged to pray and vote our conscience with no pressure to vote red or blue. Neither makes you more holy, because voting is simply your civic duty.

On the whole, these more modernized churches have removed more of what makes the Black Church what it has been to communities generation after generation—a place that was the hub and catalyst for the Civil Rights Movement, social service, Black pride, excellence, and joy; that spoke truth to power about how we should move about in this strange land where a Black woman can run for the highest office, but where health, financial, and other social disparities that threaten our personhood remain a reality. Sure, there is special emphasis during Black History Month at the nondenominational church I attended, but isn't that what they do at our jobs?

The Black Church worship experience is different, and social justice themes and emphases are one of the primary ways it differentiates itself. Certainly it is different in style—the preaching and even the big sounds of mass choirs in three- and four-part harmony singing everything from gospel music to hymns, Negro spirituals and anthems from the high-church tradition. The Black Church also veers from the path of other churches on the very basis on which the Black Church was founded: the exclusion of Black people from white churches and also, most importantly, the suffering that Black people have endured since arriving on US soil more than four hundred years ago.

In January 2025, the National Urban League reported that there had been ten Black Church fires across the United States alone, three of them in Louisiana. Those three churches were each more than one hundred years old: Greater Union Baptist Church, St. Mary Baptist Church, and Mount Pleasant Baptist Church in St. Landry Parish. The organization says that these recent Black Church burnings are a part of a spike in hate crimes in the United States since 2015 when racist rhetoric became a large part of the presidential campaign. Why Black churches have been targeted since 1822 has to do with what even white supremacists recognized: the Black Church is the heartbeat of the Black community; it serves as a spiritual, social, and political hub that represents autonomy because the Black Church is prime target for those seeking to suppress Black progress.

Suffering counterintuitively creates an environment rich in hope, anticipation, and the positive emotions that neuroscience reveals are crucial for perseverance. Historically, Black people have learned the other nine of the leadership lessons outlined in this book through a social justice emphasis—resilience, community, perseverance, faith and purpose, speaking and storytelling, collaboration, accountability, creativity and innovation, and economic empowerment—and through a liberation theology that centers the underserved. Take social justice out of the Black Church and you essentially gut it of the one primary driver of leadership development, but you especially gut the special sauce that makes the Black Church such a powerful force for change in the Black community and in the United States.

L. MICHELLE SMITH

The Social Justice of the Black Church Teaches Fairness and Empathy

There is something to be said for people who have suffered generation over generation. Not only are their worship, praise, prayers, and preaching different, they also are acutely aware of the signs of suffering in others. It feels like a natural extension to look out for the needs of others, and that is a very powerful leadership quality to have. Not only does empathy allow one to access the emotions that bridge to fairness, the ability to tap into that fairness grants a leader the ability to be just and seek justice. Empathy is a form of perspective taking, a term used in neuroscience to describe a social justice tool. It is crucial for recognizing unfairness and inequity. Historically, the Black Church has engaged storytelling, active listening, and intergenerational mentoring to instill these traits in its people. When this aspect of the Black Church experience is missing, the worship experience rings hollow for those who recognize the struggle, past and present.

More than 32 percent of the Black corporate leaders I surveyed said they learned social justice and activism from the Black Church. I thought that number would be higher, but things have changed. Xavier Williams, retired AT&T executive, current wireless CEO, and former first gentleman of a church, pointed to three primary shifts in modern-day Black churches that are turning it away from its original emphasis on social justice and thus stripping it from its original power positioning in society:

- a shift from the church being the focal point of Black lives to where church is planned around our lives and only if we choose to fit it in. "Life revolved around church when I was growing up.

Where now it feels like, you know, church revolves around your life and you'll fit it in," Williams said.

- a shift from outward compassion toward others in the form of fairness, justice, and collective liberation to a focus inward to individual prosperity, which has in many cases paralyzed the congregation from collective action because it is less involved in the service and therefore the church's missions. "A lot of churches now have become more performance-based . . . trying to set the atmosphere instead of the Holy Spirit setting the atmosphere."
- a shift away from the preacher or pastor as an aspirational figure and one of the most powerful authorities in the Black community who was capable of building coalitions and making power moves that would improve the community's condition in society. "By definition, typically, the pastor, the preacher, was one of the most powerful people in your community. It seems a lot of those things have shifted," Williams said. "I do not meet many young folks that aspire to be in the pulpit anymore. That used to be the aspiration in life for the talented tenth."

For young people to aspire to be ministers and pastors, they'd probably need to be in the building or at least streaming to see the behavior modeled before them. No doubt, there are healthy youth ministries all over the nation, but the data show that these ministries are missing a large group of young people. In a 2024 *New York Times* article titled "The Black Church Has a Gen-Z Issue: 'They Don't Come Into the Building Anymore,'" the writer explores how the Black Church is struggling to keep Gen Z in its active memberships. The article shared Gallup research that revealed that adult Black Church attendance has plunged by 20 percent over the past twenty years, with most of that drop caused by the younger generations.

While Black millennials and members of Generation Z do attend religious services, only about half attend majority-Black churches, compared with two-thirds of Black baby boomers and members of the Silent Generation, according to a Pew Research Center survey. Efforts to attract younger attendees to the Black Church have been a struggle.

"Older Black churchgoers lament the church's declining membership, worried that the great generational chain of inheritance has been broken, imperiling the civil and voting rights legacy they've created. And they are confounded by the cultural divides that make it difficult to reach younger members of their community," *Times* reporter Clyde McGrady asserts.

One reason why younger Black Americans aren't attending Black Church services in person is that they no longer view the Black Church as the central hub in the fight for social justice, and that is unfortunate because according to the article, younger generations have an expressed desire to be involved in social justice and activism. They know the stories of Martin Luther King Jr. and the Civil Rights Movement, but for them it seems so long ago and out of reach. They also witnessed many Black Church leaders criticize the Black Lives Matter movement, which left them feeling alone and not supported. Technology has allowed young people to stay connected with their faith or spirituality because of streaming services and the presence of faith organizations on social media and podcasts, but technology is also standing between young Black people of faith and the pews. Tech has made faith and spirituality convenient and accessible. They can watch on demand any day of the week, and on Sunday, they can swipe through the nation's church services and cherry-pick where they virtually attend with as many choices as any dating app could produce. The pandemic accelerated the separation of younger Black generations from the sanctuary as well. "Black Protestants are especially likely to attend virtual services and are more likely to cite COVID as a reason, according to Pew.... Of those regularly attending virtually, 42 percent say they felt a 'great deal' of connection to the in-person service, compared with 72 percent of those attending in person," McGrady writes.

The *Times* article concluded that this demographic shift for the Black Church had major implications for the Black community's social cohesion and political power within social justice efforts. The Black Church historically played a central role in leadership development. Older generations see the Black Church as a hub for mentorship, activism, and community organizing, whereas younger generations seek these roles in nonreligious spaces, like on TikTok or even podcasts.

It can be surmised that if you have fewer young people in the Black Church, fewer future Black leaders will be shaped by the church's influence on leadership in secular spaces, like in the business realm. This shift raises questions about where Black leadership will be cultivated in the future, especially as rollbacks on affirmative action and diversity, equity, and inclusion in universities and private and public industry take hold. In that 2024 *New York Times* article, which was published just before the 2024 presidential election, the writer explores how the disconnect that Gen Z is experiencing with the Black Church could likely impact the outcome.

I stumbled on one of those young Black men on TikTok who was raised by his grandmother and attended church like I did: a couple of times during the week, on Saturdays for youth meetings and events, and then all day and evening on Sunday from Sunday School in the morning to Baptist Training Union in the evening. His posts intrigued me because not only could I relate to him, he was also well read and studied about religion, Black culture, the Black Church, and hip-hop. He spit out line after line of wisdom that sounded like it came from someone twice his age while mixing in lines from the likes of Kendrick Lamar and Rakim, but as I dug deeper into his timeline, I discovered that he was inspired enough by the Black Church to go to seminary, but turned off enough to turn his back on a dream of becoming a pastor himself. Eventually, he found himself completely deconstructing his faith, and especially the teachings and rituals that he encountered from his many years as an active participant in the Black Church. Only a week before the TikTok ban was to take effect, he emerged on my timeline once more to talk about his relationship with the Black Church; he mentioned that he was quoted in the *Times* article cited here. To be clear, Donnell McLachlan actually rejected a physical pulpit and turned the internet into a virtual one instead, because this brother still preaches. With about 350,000 followers tuning in on TikTok, McLachlan discusses his brand of post-churched faith and Black Church religion, largely deconstructing the white supremacy, misogyny, and colonialism often intertwined with it. He introduced his channel in 2021 by saying, "Hi, everyone! My name is Donnell, and welcome to Religious Studies and Decolonization TikTok! I'm glad you're here." And with a hearty laugh, he indicated that he knew he was opening the door to a discourse that would likely rock the boat and the internet. At some point, he realized, after being deeply involved in the Black Church, that all of his cousins were no longer there in the pews with him, and when the pandemic came, he, like so many, had time to sit with his thoughts. In 2021, he left the church. I reached out to him as I had in the past by private message after he posted his last TikTok before the ban deadline; I needed to get permission to link to some of his commentary for a *HuffPost* "Voices" article I was writing on an outspoken Black woman's ability to be likable in the workplace. He agreed to speak with me about the state of social justice and the Black Church, and the exodus of young Black people from it.

"They don't see the church as a place that's necessary for the kind of life they want to live," McLachlan said. "It's not where their friends are. It's not where the answers are."

The *Times* article missed something that will continue to keep young Black people away: many people have experienced trauma at the hands of the Black Church; some people minimize that trauma by branding it "church hurt." If you've been deeply hurt by someone you truly loved, would you fight with him or her for causes no matter how important and vital? Likely not. To be fair, many have experienced trauma at the hands of the people in the Black Church, and while some stay, during those times of grief, pain, and even recovery, many don't have the energy or will to fight. So, often good church people are silenced.

McLachlan said he felt as if he couldn't ask the hard questions when he was a dedicated churchgoer, and he emphasized the urgency for churches to evolve in order to remain a meaningful force in the lives of young people.

"If the church can't speak to what they're dealing with—mental health, identity, justice—it will become irrelevant to them," he said.

The Dual Mission of the Black Church

Recently, my daughter and I decided to again stream our Sunday morning worship because she had to cheer at an early afternoon basketball game. We decided against attending the early morning service in person because Sunday has become one of the days when we can sleep in a bit, but this morning's online church would be a little different. We streamed the services of two different churches because I like the praise and worship at one and the preaching at the other. I didn't realize that this would become a bit of a social experiment for me. It happened to be the Sunday before the inauguration of the forty-seventh president of the United States, which ironically was also the day before we were to celebrate the Martin Luther King Jr. holiday. We had found ourselves on the eve of nonsense because the two men couldn't represent more polar opposite ideals. So how would the two churches handle what was in the cultural ether for our country? Both churches shared moving video tributes to the civil rights leader. One hosted a panel immediately following with King's son Martin Luther King III, going deeper into how we can observe the holiday and also take King's vision into the next four years, acknowledging the foreboding felt by Black people. The other church pivoted nearly immediately to acknowledging the inauguration and asked the congregation to pray for the country's leadership.

Now, in any other election cycle, this would make sense, no matter what your party affiliation. But on the Sunday before the day that happens to be MLK Day *and* the inauguration of someone who embodies everything opposite of what King stood for, that was really some wild and tone-deaf work. I did notice that there was very little response from the congregation that routinely does not shy away from a little call and response.

It's extremely difficult to hold up the mantle of the Black Church, which is historically steeped in liberation theology, when you're willing to mention fairness in one breath and then in the next choke the breath right out of a message of hope and fairness.

To do so before a congregation, a people that are only a few generations from slavery, seems egregious. Freedom really is at the core of the Gospel itself and how our ancestors, the enslaved people, connected with it.

"It is the word, liberty, which describes the essence of the Black church and its role in the politics of equality," writes Robert S. Harvey in a 2010 article titled "Restoring the Social Justice Identity of the Black Church," which appears in *Inquiries Journal of Social Sciences, Arts, and Humanities*. He argues that the Black Church once stood as a beacon and a haven for its people, a place where they could address their spiritual needs as well as any social, political, and economic issues within the Black community. He proclaims the Black Church had a distinct dual purpose to set Black souls and bodies free through sharing the Word of God while addressing social and systemic justice issues. He questions whether the Black Church has lost its footing as the one place its people can go to experience that, that perhaps it has lost its identity in favor of messages that lean more toward self-help and prosperity and personal wealth-building and gain.

The Black Church, through its social justice tradition, provides a person with a moral compass—one that is spiritual and distinctly human. If you can't learn social justice or fairness in a Black Church, or at least learn its sensibilities so that you can share it with others, what on earth is the Black Church doing? When I was young, there were times when we went to church and the pastor's core topic might be about a current event, and he would use scripture to support his expository preaching. I recall one Sunday in particular that happened to be the one before Super Bowl XXII, where Doug Williams of the then Washington Redskins (now more appropriately called the Commanders) became the first Black quarterback to lead an NFL team to victory. It was one more major victory for Black people in

America, because the quarterback position was most often reserved for white players because of racial stereotyping. There was the belief that a white player would not follow the lead of a Black player or that Black players weren't intelligent enough to pull off the position; the feeling was that the quarterback leveraged more brains than brawn. Black players in other positions like running back, wide receiver, or defensive end were stereotyped to have amazing physicality, but that was it. A 2015 study by Brian Volz found that even when Black men secured the role of quarterback, they were often benched. The first Black quarterback in the NFL was a man named Fritz Pollard; he was appointed in 1923, but he rarely played. It took nearly one hundred years for the NFL to routinely start a Black quarterback, and even that was somewhat of a fluke. When Geno Smith stepped up to fill in for an injured Eli Manning in 2017, he represented the 25 percent of starting quarterbacks who were Black. Arguably, the turning point could have come in 1988 when Doug Williams became the first Black quarterback to start and subsequently win the Super Bowl. He threw for 340 yards and four touchdowns, which was a record for that time; he was also named Super Bowl MVP. I still remember him turning to the camera and saying, "I'm going to Disney World!" We'd never seen anything like it before. So dramatic was that victory for Williams, the Washington Redskins, and Black people in general that my pastor Dr. C. A. W. Clark preached one of his most noted and most listened-to sermons of that time. The sermon was called "The Game Is Fixed." It wasn't odd for these stories to take over the pulpit when our people had seemingly overcome. In fact, we expected it. It also wasn't odd for preachers to center the crises that we faced as a people in sermons. Social chatter among Black people in general points toward this. Let something happen in the news that concerns

Black people, and predictably, someone will post, "I wonder how the Black pastors will handle this one on Sunday?"

So, it was so odd to me to see negative chatter on social media after the devastating results of the 2024 election when my pastor preached a sermon called "A Letter to Black Women." He again centered the current event but supported his message with scripture throughout. I remember seeing a TikTok video and a Thread from a young Black woman who happened to visit the church and decided to log a two-minute video review of the church. She entered anticipating a good time. She loved the praise and worship, but the sermon turned her off. She said that it was a "motivational speech," and that she had gone to church to hear the Word, not attend what she described as "a mourning for Vice President Kamala Harris." She told her viewers that if they wanted to hear the Word, not to attend that church. Clearly not a part of the 92 percent of Black women who voted for Kamala Harris, but also not someone who was accustomed to or had knowledge of the deep history of the Black Church. The Black Church is the keeper of all things Black history and social justice, yet this young woman, although she seemed ultra-"saved," also seemed to me to be so lost. Why was it that a pastor couldn't minister to the 92 percent of Black women and even the 81 percent of Black men who voted for Harris and felt a sense of betrayal and hopelessness? Why was that so out of line? From the looks of it, the woman seemed to be a member of Gen Z, and was likely exposed to churches that did not center liberation as core to its message or identity. It's also very possible that she was used to attending white or multicultural churches. There is also a great chance that she had only been in church for a short time before her visit. The fact that someone can offer a church review of any substance with one visit in a two-minute video is nearly as disturbing.

The Modernization of the Black Church and the Decentering of Social Justice

There is a slight nuance between justice leadership and social justice leadership that's worth noting. Justice leadership focuses on fairness, following the rules and exercising impartiality in the decision-making process. Social justice in leadership takes the concept of justice further.

Another reason that many churches have strayed from a core focus on social justice lies in their attempts to modernize their services and welcome those who come from other church traditions where the themes were not a part of their journey. I believe that this is at least part of the modernization of the Black Church. One executive I interviewed told me I was using code when I called it modernization, and said that what I really meant was that some Black churches are trying to be white. There are indeed other aspects to this modernization, but in some cases, these churches are indeed accommodating for a growing number of white and brown congregants.

Centering social justice can also make your church a target. Social justice to some is synonymous with politics. Perhaps this came into clearer focus with the dawn of social media and streaming of church services. Who can forget when then-Senator Barack Obama made his first run for president and, during the primaries as he ran against Senator Hillary Clinton, news broke of a worship service where Obama's pastor at the time, Rev. Jeremiah Wright, was preaching what many would argue were themes they'd heard on any given Sunday in any Black church. But because Obama was largely running as a post-racial candidate for the president of the United States and the church that he was attending at the time was in line with the Black Church tradition where liberation theology took main stage every Sunday, conflict arose. That is, if anyone ever connected the dots between the candidate and his church's worldview. A decade before, and they likely wouldn't have unless the candidate himself was a preacher, like Jesse Jackson. However, as many Black churches began to do on Sundays in the early 2000s, worship services were streamed online or at least recorded and posted on YouTube. As a result, there was one certain sermon that was laid bare for the masses to scrutinize because the now-famous Democratic candidate for president of the United States was a faithful member of the Trinity United Church of Christ in Chicago, Illinois, where Wright was senior pastor at the time. Obama was having a pretty successful run as he was performing well in the caucuses and primaries, that is, until he was on his way to Pennsylvania when the media obtained a video of Wright's preaching. Had they ever even heard a pastor use a four-letter word in the pulpit? Plenty of Black people have, especially from their Black Baptist preachers, and if you ask Jeremiah Wright, he wasn't the first to say it in the context of damning America for injustices at home and abroad. What exactly did he say? Imagine waking up to *Good Morning America* and seeing the video of Wright preaching hellfire and brimstone on the United States while saying this:

"The government gives them the drugs, builds bigger prisons, passes a three-strike law, and then wants us to sing 'God Bless America.' No, no, no, not God Bless America. God damn America—that's in the Bible—for killing innocent people. God damn America, for treating our citizens as less than human."

The sound bite was playing everywhere, on local and national news, late-night talk shows and morning magazines, and it even became viral on social media seemingly overnight. The right began calling Wright antiwhite, and because this pastor married the Obamas and they attended this church, the question tossed around the most was whether Obama was "a radical." It didn't seem to matter that Obama was not in attendance the Sunday Wright preached this sermon. The general public, mainly modern white America, had little to no context, cultural or otherwise, for what was being said in the Black Church Sunday to Sunday until perhaps this fateful inflection point in the historic Obama campaign. Many believe that this incident alone could have completely derailed his run for the high office. Wright's message sounded anti-American to them, and to some, incredibly unpatriotic, even prejudiced because it centered Black people and their liberty above all. The publicity was so bad for Obama that his campaign had to go to great lengths to recover from the negative news coverage the ordeal produced. Senator Obama chose to take the opportunity to address the nation on race and approach the issue in a more nuanced way. On March 18, 2008, Obama delivered a speech that he wrote himself called "A More Perfect Union," which not only cemented him as the right candidate to move forward in the election for president but also confirmed the role of the Black Church as an institution that had the right and the mission to speak on issues of race and injustice. The speech has been heralded as the most prolific speech on race since Martin Luther King Jr.'s "I Have a Dream" speech.

"The profound mistake of Reverend Wright's sermons is not that he spoke about racism in our society. It's that he spoke as if our society was static; as if no progress had been made," said Obama. Behind the scenes, this did cause friction between the two; however, he did not immediately turn his back on his pastor, his words, or the liberation doctrine that defines the Black Church. He used biblical language alongside constitutional language to call for transformation in our country, quoting Luke 4:18–19: "To bring Good News to the poor . . . to proclaim that captives will be released . . . that the oppressed will be set free." In this way he affirmed the core freedom theology of the Black Church. Unlike his critics who wanted him to disavow what Wright said or even, more broadly, the stance of his or any Black Church that centers pointed critiques of racial injustice in our country, Obama embraced it as an opportunity to begin a dialogue about how to change the harsh realities Black Americans face while acknowledging the frustrations of white Americans who were also struggling in our society, albeit in different ways. Bridging back to themes of hope and change, Obama nearly talked his way out of a political disaster that had the potential to not only undo his campaign but also undermine an institution that ultimately led him to Christ.

However, the bad press continued. It was also unrelenting for Rev. Wright, but he didn't take it personally. He later told the National Press Club that the attacks from the public against him were actually attacks on the Black Church. Wright made more remarks at that press conference that caused the ire of even some in the Black Church, but ultimately he called Obama a politician because he said that Obama was privately agreeing with him and publicly distancing himself. Wright had a face-to-face conversation with Obama, who asked him to stop preaching until after the election. Wright disagreed. Some years later, Wright shared the details of one of the final conversations the two would have on the HBO documentary *Obama: In Pursuit of a More Perfect Union*. Obama said to him, "You know what your problem is? As a preacher, you have to speak the truth." Wright responded, "Well, that's a good problem to have."

By April, the relationship was so fraught, Obama went public with his intent to cut ties with his pastor, according to a 2008 *New York Times* article. The softer stance he took in his earlier speech dissipated. He made it clear that his twenty-year relationship with the pastor who baptized his two daughters had come to an end. Barack Obama's break from Rev. Jeremiah Wright was indeed a political maneuver, but it was also a defining moment etched into the soul of American history. It laid bare the deep and often irreconcilable tension between Black secular and political leadership and the uncompromising moral force of the Black Church. In that moment, Obama was not just a candidate; he was a man navigating the chasm between righteousness and pragmatism, between loyalty and legacy, between prophetic truth and the price of power.

Black Church Modernization Clashes Head-On with the Prophetic Tradition

This incident caused many Black churches to take a long look at how technology might require them to temper their tradition of prophetic sermons or, conversely, pull the plug on online church or posting recordings on YouTube. Most Black churches soldiered forward into the digital world and held on to the Black Church tradition of upholding social justice as a core value, deciding that this watershed moment simply meant that more people would be exposed to their message. If there was something extremely sensitive to be discussed, that leadership was ill-prepared to explore with a broader audience, it would be postponed for other meetings or communications that were less public. In some cases, cameras would stop rolling or the AV team would edit the service or sermon before it was posted online. Now, following the pandemic shutdown, most churches that facilitate online services have become so savvy with the technology they are able to walk this line without stirring the pot with the masses. Of course, it helps if you don't have a presidential candidate in your membership, but many political leaders indeed attend Black churches.

But what leadership lesson is there for those professionals in the corporate and business realms? The ability to call out what is wrong is something that Black leaders know how to do, and sometimes with the smooth political savvy of a practiced politician. However, sometimes, because Black leaders are the only ones in a room, on a corporate jet, or in a boardroom with opponents who may decenter and other us, we might find the occasion to stand "ten toes down," make the pictures shake on the wall, and call "a thing a thing." The prophetic tradition in the Black Church speaks to the fiery callouts and calls to action from the pulpit to those in the world who may be burdening, holding captive, or holding back a people; and of course in Black America's early years, enslaving them; or throughout Jim Crow or the civil rights era, brutalizing, impeding access, or continuing to move the goalpost on progress. Prophetic, in this sense, does not speak to a person's ability to foretell the future. It speaks to the brash, rude, and sometimes untamed manner in which the person delivers harsh truths.

In a PBS interview shortly after the Wright-Obama upheaval, Dr. Harold Dean Trulear, a professor of applied theology at the Howard University School of Divinity in Washington, spoke with a PBS anchor to deconstruct what the nation had witnessed and talk about its relevance to the Black Church. The anchor asked about the validity of saying that Wright was in the prophetic tradition when on some points the anchor called him "wildly wrong and mistaken" while using profanity and making incendiary comments.

"Well, many people thought the biblical prophets were wildly wrong and mistaken," Trulear said. "Many people thought that Jesus was wildly wrong and mistaken. So that alone would not be sufficient to dissuade people from emulating him as a prophet." In the prophetic tradition, Trulear called Wright an exemplar.

Think of Elijah, an Old Testament prophet. The man the Bible describes as fierce, dramatic, and fearless. Prophets in the Bible weren't always what most thought of as presentable either. In the New Testament, John the Baptist lived in the wild and wore clothes made of camel's hair and lunched on locusts. Ezekiel was also a piece of work, incredibly unconventional. At one point he ate a scroll to prove a point. He shaved his head and beard as an omen, and even preached to dry bones. Then there was Jeremiah, who called Israel a spiritual adulterer and smashed a clay pot before the leaders as a symbol of their coming judgment from God. Sound like another Jeremiah? He was ultimately thrown in jail and beaten, but he kept preaching anyway.

In short, the prophetic tradition isn't pretty, but it is the kind of call from a pulpit that will no doubt receive a response from a congregation because of the boldness to say what probably needed to be said all week by churchgoers, but couldn't be for fear of retribution. Either you temper your words at work or at school or at the store, or you stay silent. Or perhaps it was a tough truth that no one really wanted to hear. I remember one elderly preacher I heard say, "Draw up your feet! I'm coming through!" It was his way of saying, I'm about to step on your toes with this truth. Hold on to your hymnals! The sheer bravery of these Black pastors to speak truth to power, to say what everyone else wants to and can't, then sometimes yell it out, scream it, or whoop it out, is just what Black congregants need to validate their emotions and their plight. So is the prophetic tradition something that is a direct lesson for corporate leaders? The application can't be the same, as was so starkly demonstrated in the Wright-Obama debacle. Obama's relationship to that prophetic tradition caused the broader world to question him as the calm, cool, collected unifier he attempted to be and would eventually become. It could be argued that hearing someone scream out from the pulpit the thing that you know you can't say as someone in the corporate or political world might be just the sanctuary and salve one's corporate soul needs to go back into the corporate towers and lead with the grace that has become expected of us.

The prophetic tradition within the Black Church provides significant benefits to its leaders by offering a platform that empowers them

- to speak out against social and racial injustice,
- to advocate for change,
- to cling to a sense of hope and agency,
- to serve as a crucial tool for resistance against oppression, particularly during slavery and the Civil Rights Movement,
- to act as a voice for the marginalized, giving them a sense of empowerment to fight for their rights.

Rev. Cokiesha Bailey Robinson, associate dean of mentoring and cross cultural engagement at Grace College, an author, and an ordained minister, was firm in her belief that there is a renewed urgency for the Black Church as a whole to reclaim its prophetic tradition. She called on Black churches to reclaim their prophetic role—speaking truth to power, confronting systemic injustice, and embodying a hope deeply rooted in historical memory. She likened the Black Church's return to the centering of social justice as one of its core leadership lessons, and that it was paramount.

Rev. Robinson eloquently framed the prophetic tradition as a call to memory, action, and spiritual renewal, especially in the wake of the 2024 election results that threatened to challenge Black Americans and those who are called to lead inside and outside of the Black Church. She stated: "Hope is rooted in a long memory that returns in dreams, songs, sermonic cadence, and dancing in the fire of the Holy Ghost that brings life. But this long, lingering memory must be retrieved and embodied in practices that congregate, conjure, and conspire in the contemporary life worlds of those who have been dismissed and left behind in a world of globalized capital."

Drawing from Ezekiel's vision of dry bones, she declared that only the power of the Holy Ghost can revive, renew, and resurrect Black churches in this defining moment of history.

"Behold, the bones in our post-racialized valley of the twenty-first century are very dry, and nothing less than the Holy Ghost can breathe life that revives and renews and resurrects Black churches from this moment to which history has called us."

Rev. Robinson cautioned that if scholars and church leaders fail to remember, retell, and relive these prophetic stories, Black churches risk being trapped in post-racial illusions and hollow egalitarian promises. Rev. Robinson urged a return to liberation theology—one that transcends stagnant doctrine and breathes life into the ongoing struggle for justice.

The Prophetic Tradition of the Black Church Rewires Our Brains for Bravery

More than anything, the prophetic tradition of preachers offers an undying model of bravery and courage in the face of incredible odds. Because those odds haven't been as steep as those in the civil rights era or even before then during Jim Crow and slavery, perhaps the Black Church has veered into more individualistic themes of self-empowerment and prosperity because it hasn't been faced with the same perils. Perhaps what presents itself in 2025 might just bring the Black Church back to a time when fiery calls for fairness, equality, and justice help us rewire our brains and put fear in its rightful place—the fuel for courage itself. Neuroscience says that bravery is a result of a complex interaction between the amygdala, which is our brain's fear center for fight, flight, or freeze, and the prefrontal cortex, where we make executive decisions. These are the primary areas that are activated, but there is also a mix of actions from smaller, lesser known areas of the brain that make this happen. Think of it as the brain's bravery gospel quintet, singing backup to those main areas of the brain, harmonizing to big impact:

- **Ventral midline thalamus (vMT):** What some scientists have called the "brain switch" for courage, receives information from other brain areas and sends it to the amygdala and prefrontal cortex

- **Subgenual anterior cingulate cortex (sgACC):** Suppresses fear responses
- **Right temporal pole (rTP):** Processes emotions, social cues, and language
- **Insula:** Processes emotions, performs interoception, and assesses risks
- **Hippocampus:** Helps form memories associated with courageous actions

Then there is the potent chemical cocktail that is stirred up by this activity in our brains: dopamine, which gives us a boost of positive emotion and encouragement to keep going and ask for more; serotonin, which calms us in the midst of it all; and adrenaline, also known as epinephrine, which is the chemical known to give mothers the superpowers they need to jump into action to save their babies when they are in peril. All of this causes our brains to reframe fear. And there you have the power of the Black Church. It stokes bravery through the most treacherous times for its people.

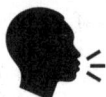

THE LEADERSHIP LESSONS

Social justice as a leadership responsibility. While business leaders are generally not activists, they have a duty to advocate for fairness and justice, not just within their organizations but in society at large. Corporate and civic leaders should embrace social consciousness as part of leadership, ensuring their organizations reflect values of equity, inclusion, and responsibility toward marginalized communities, engaging perspective taking and empathy wherever possible.

The power of the prophetic voice inspires courage. Effective leaders speak truth to power even when it is uncomfortable or risky. In the corporate world, leaders must develop the courage to challenge unfair practices within their companies, industries, and society, even when there is resistance.

Social justice strengthens leadership resilience. The struggles of marginalized communities cultivate resilience, adaptability, and a solutions-driven mindset—all critical leadership traits. Leaders who have faced adversity can use those experiences to fuel innovation, strategic thinking, and long-term vision in their industries.

Social justice engages future generations of leaders. Young leaders want to engage with organizations that will act in a values-driven fashion, but if institutions fail to support their passion for the greater good, they will look elsewhere. Companies and organizations should ensure they provide spaces where people of younger generations feel empowered to lead, speak out, and advocate for change.

Social justice is a leadership mandate. Social justice is not just a moral obligation—it is a leadership principle that fuels resilience, courage, perseverance, social cohesion, and collective empowerment. Whether in corporate settings, community leadership, or personal advocacy, the lessons of the Black Church's social justice legacy can help leaders drive meaningful, systemic change.

COACHING QUESTIONS

How does your leadership reflect a commitment to justice and equity, and in what ways could you take a stronger stand on issues that affect marginalized communities?

Think of a time when you witnessed or experienced injustice in your workplace or community. How did you respond, and what might you do differently next time to be a more effective advocate?

The prophetic voice in the Black Church has long been a source of courage and truth-telling, and it rewires our brains for bravery. How can you incorporate boldness and integrity into your leadership while balancing the realities of corporate or institutional constraints?

What steps can you take to ensure that the next generation of leaders—especially those from underrepresented backgrounds—is empowered to use their voices for the values about which they are passionate?

9
CREATIVITY AND INNOVATION
Miracles and Blessings

If you've ever been to a small rural town, the kind that has one stoplight and you can't drive too fast down the highway because you may just miss the town completely, you're probably familiar with how everyone knows the homecoming queen by her first and last name because she is the mayor's daughter. The mayor is also the pastor and the chief of police, and he owns the grocery store and both gas stations. That was a young Cynthia "Cynt" Marshall, retired Dallas Mavericks CEO and former AT&T executive, when she began her involvement with the Black Church. From the time she first remembers, all the way through her young adult years, Cynt held several roles in ministry. She preached. She was the vice president of the choir. She was a Sunday School teacher. She was even a youth director and an usher. When she was vice president of the New Bethel Youth Choir in the late 1970s, the group cut an album called *Heaven*.

In each of her leadership roles, Cynt added an extra flourish that included either music, props, or costumes, much like when she delivers a message today. She gets the crowd warmed up with a line dance, passes out tiaras, or closes her message with an inspiring sing-a-long of Marvin Gaye and Tammi Terrell's "Ain't No Mountain High Enough." Adding a splash of creativity to boost engagement or bring home a message is her signature, and she says it started when she was a young leader in the Black Church. She was named youth director at the age of twenty-two, the youngest to be named to the position in that church, which was planted by a chosen group from New Bethel Apostolic Holy Church. Those young people she was in charge of were in for a treat.

"One time we did this whole program where we were studying Abraham and I said, no, we're not going to just study it," she said. "We're going to dress up in character. It was a big youth program. We looked like we were back in the Bible, because that's what you do. And it made people really get into their character. It would get so emotional."

In addition to big productions, Cynt also planned off-site, well-chaperoned retreats for the youth at one of the nearby Embassy Suites hotels, where she featured workshops and fun activities that not only taught scriptural principles but featured skating field trips and other fun outings. Cynt also featured career and résumé development sessions.

"I would have them doing all kinds of stuff. I would have them writing. We would have workshops on writing," she said. "I got a little bit more deliberate [with the leadership lessons], because it was infused.... We even had graduation ceremonies. So, everybody would march in, in their caps and gowns. I'd go rent all these caps and gowns, and they'd march in."

This creativity and innovation carried over into her work as a senior executive. Beyond supercharging a packed ballroom for the industry-leading AT&T ERG Conference with the message "diversity is being invited to the party while inclusion is being invited to dance," she ended it in a round of the "Cupid Shuffle" where she invited everyone to dance. Cynt has been known to surprise and delight employees in ways they never really expected. It's the kind of delight that if repeated again and again while delivering on promises brings entire organizations back to life. I quipped with her that it was like Easter at the Dallas Mavericks' organization. No more dark clouds; the organization came back to life after she unleashed her magic.

When she rolled out her one-hundred-day plan for the Mavericks and executed it, she also directed a complete renovation of the offices, where workers painted illustrations of each of the values and the mission on the walls. She kept the illustrations covered until shortly before the completion of the one hundred days.

"They were not used to that kind of workplace, right? And it was all different quotes people had said. And then they walked in, and we had a station where everybody had to dip their hands in this gray paint and press them onto the walls. And we got this big white wall in the back and basically said, 'Are you all in?'" she said. "People literally started crying just because we cared enough to make sure they were up on that wall."

The Black Church Is Where They Put Sauce on It

When people saw the Super Bowl LIX halftime show with Kendrick Lamar, they saw a Pulitzer Prize–winning artist unraveling a multilayered message for the times at the most-watched cultural event in our nation. I saw that too, don't get me wrong, but what jumped out at me most was the Black Church allusions throughout, especially the choir march Kendrick led as he ushered in that one diss track that made the fans in the stadium and most of the record-breaking viewership lose their minds—"Not Like Us." In that performance there is a singular clip of Kendrick and the "angels," the female dancers that served as his conscience throughout the performance, whispering in his ear to consider things before he proceeded, marching in like the church usher board. Social media creators replaced the "Not Like Us" track with familiar gospel tunes like those from John P. Kee and other 1990s mass choir tunes. The irony was they didn't have to do anything to the video to sync it to Kendrick's moves. He and the angels were right on beat.

Visions of ushers marching in syncopation to the beat of a gospel song, or even hundreds of choir members in their choir robes swishing and swaying from the double doors at the entrance of the church, down the center aisle, taking their sweet time and vamping the song multiple times before finally arriving in the choir stand in their places thirty minutes later, is something you'd witness only in the Black Church. Somehow, Black business executives inhaled it into their lungs, metabolized it within their bodies at the cellular level, and spread it into corporate spaces with ease, grace, and plenty of onlookers who want to join in or cheer it on.

It's the sauce.

In fact, Carla Harris said that the improvisation or riffing that you witness in the Black Church is rich with leadership lessons. The choir riffs when the director takes it in new directions based on the response she or he is getting from the congregation. The soloist improvises as she or he looks for ways in the moment to get the right emotions across or emphasize words that invoke the Spirit. Even the preacher may ad-lib, veering off his or her outline so that his or her sermon goes where the Spirit leads and so that the congregation is moved. In short, the Black Church teaches you at every turn what it is to extemporize or, as Harris called it, "pivot." The culture of the Black Church, collectively, is highly emotional because there is an innate ability to read the room, adjust and move forward, and do it smoothly.

Harris embodies this in her ability to adjust her tone, delivery, and message and even her songs based on the environment. That Baptist youth choir incursion by a thirteen-year-old Catholic set her on a path to prestigious concert halls and corporate boardrooms.

"At my very first concert in 2005 at Carnegie Hall, I had rehearsed fourteen songs. But when I got to the twelfth song, I knew I was on top of the mountain. That was my crescendo," she said. "You're like, Where am I going from here? Everything in me said, 'Carla, if you sing one more note, you're going to be on the other side of that mountain.' So, I looked at that audience. They were standing on their feet," she continued. "They were so happy, smiles everywhere. I said, 'Good night, everybody!' And my choir and my band was like, 'Whoa, whoa, we got two songs.' I said, 'Good night, everybody!' Because I knew it was over. I knew it; I could feel it."

She has taken that sensibility with her onto speaking platforms in the corporate realm where she wields her other superpower, speaking. Knowing when to pivot in the middle of a message is also a sensibility that she has picked up from the Black Church, especially from singing and leading the choir.

"Sometimes somebody contracts me for an hour: forty to forty-five minutes of content and fifteen to twenty minutes of Q&A," she said. "But if I feel that I've done all I can with that audience for thirty-eight minutes, I don't push it. I say to myself, 'I'm prepared to give the money back.' But thirty-eight minutes and then I go to a Q&A. So that ability to be in tune with your audience and to pivot quickly. I'm like, 'That's it.' Yeah, I've gotten there. This is all I need to do."

The ability to "read the room," as some call it, opens up the opportunity for creativity, but it also hones emotional intelligence, yielding highly empathetic next moves based on what the room requires.

"Because everybody values being heard. So, one of the things that I say a lot today in my speeches is, you want to serve the room. You don't want to focus so much on selling," she said. "Because they may or may not be in the mood to be sold, but everybody's in the mood to be served. And when you say, 'I'm listening to you; I want to hear you,' and then you do that, you engage in a way that's going to be valuable."

Leaders who are in tune with others and can adapt to change on a dime are creative and innovative leaders. According to an essay by Emmanuel Agbor, "Creative leaders are able to embrace change and to encourage followers to question why the organization does things in a certain way, and then seek out alternative ways of doing things. These leaders treat mistakes as part of the learning process and do not punish followers who try new ideas and fail. Therefore, they help create organizational cultures where people can take risks and even make mistakes."

Creativity Taps into Intuition, Which Abounds in the Black Church

Creative leaders can feel their way through challenges; they aren't simply in their heads. I recall the first few times I led praise and worship at Concord Church. It was a bit different from leading a solo in front of the mass choir, which is what I did while growing up at Good Street Baptist Church. There you only really had to look at the congregation and watch the director out of the corner of your eye. Sometimes, the director would follow you; other times, you'd follow him or her. Leading praise and worship was different. Everyone depended on you, not only the congregation, but the praise and worship team behind you, the band and the choir. Our minister of music rotated leadership responsibilities to each of us, so at least one Sunday out of the month, one of us was in charge of the entire praise and worship set, which was a huge responsibility. It was up to that week's leader to usher in the presence of the Lord for thousands of people at once while the pastor and staff looked on. No pressure, right?

Some Sundays we'd pass the mic. That meant that if there were three songs in the set, your team member may lead one, someone else might lead the other, and you may lead the third. On one particular Sunday, I led the second song. I never will forget that the person who led ahead of me really got the congregation going with this one song. It was one of my favorites from the Brooklyn Tabernacle Choir, but the song I was to lead afterward was more of a slower-tempo worship tune. As she wrapped with a vamp that had the band cooking and the congregation on its feet, I couldn't imagine slowing them down to zero so suddenly. What I did next surprised my teammates, and I'll admit it surprised me too. I'd never been in this situation, but my intuition told me what needed to be done. When Felicia passed me the mic, I waited for the break, and I started ad-libbing the vamp again and motioned to the band.

For some context, I should pause in the story and share more about the cultural reference for "the break," which came from DJ and hip-hop culture and not the church, although many a church musician gained their chops by playing in both church and club venues. Like most Black Church music and R&B/Soul music, there's a bit of a chicken and egg scenario happening. Think The Clark Sisters' "You Brought the Sunshine" and Stevie Wonder's "Master Blaster (Jammin')" or even go back further to Mahalia Jackson infusing jazz and blues influences into her gospel music. You could flip that and look at how artists like Aretha Franklin had a heavy gospel influence, which is why it's called Soul music. We probably didn't get that same sustained effect in hip-hop until Kirk Franklin came onto the scene. However, Kurtis Blow rapped about "The Breaks," in 1980, a pun if you will, meaning the breaks you have when you get a reprieve from hard times or wins in between them. He was also referencing the breaks that come in the music between the beats when DJs know to cut a song, scratch, or go to the next song in a set. You know it because you feel it, and the entire room reacts. In an unconscious nod to the Black Church tradition, the song features a call-and-response style, echoing the way break dancers would interact with the crowd and the DJ. In any case, Rev

Run, Blow's original DJ, would have been proud of me when I engaged a break in church.

The congregation was right there with me, so was the band, and we went for another three minutes, and I slowed that song down until I knew the room was ready to sing softly and lift holy hands. This was not something you'd see at Good Street, and nothing I'd ever done before, but I knew I could do it, and I knew it had to be done. So, I did it. No one expected that from the classically trained mezzo-soprano from Good Street Baptist Church.

Leadership is like that sometimes. You have to take the people where you know they need to go, even if no one else sees it coming. You also have to take risks, do things you've never done before, stretch yourself, and have the confidence to make it happen to the best of your ability. When it was time to take our seats, I clearly remember Felicia hugging me from the side saying, "You started that song up again and slowed it down! That was so good!"

Creativity is a game-changer for leaders, no matter the industry. It's about thinking beyond the obvious, solving tough problems in new ways, and inspiring others to push past limitations. In a world that's constantly shifting, creativity helps leaders stay ahead—adapting, seizing fresh opportunities, and driving lasting success.

A truly creative leader doesn't just innovate; they build a culture where new ideas thrive. When teams feel empowered to think differently, they approach challenges with fresh perspectives, strengthening the organization as a whole. By embracing creativity, leaders sharpen their strategic vision, foster continuous growth, and create an environment where originality isn't just encouraged—it's expected.

Creativity in leadership is multifaceted, and it can have a deep impact on organizational success. The fundamental aspects of creativity in leadership include:

Innovative Thinking: The ability to conceive and implement new ideas and approaches that drive progress. Creative leaders demonstrate an openness to new ideas and a dedication to creating an environment of innovation and experimentation within their teams.

Problem-Solving: Using creative strategies to address and overcome complex challenges. Creative problem-solving is a leadership approach that involves using innovative thinking, adaptability, and collaboration to generate effective solutions.

Visionary Leadership: Envisioning future possibilities and guiding the organization toward them with creativity. Creative leadership is demonstrated when leaders leverage creativity, innovation, and the disruption of conventional patterns to break new ground.

Encouraging Collaboration: Fostering a collaborative environment where diverse ideas can flourish. To foster a culture of creativity, leaders should lead by example, encourage diverse teams, provide training and development, reward and recognize innovation, and promote cross-functional collaboration.

Adaptability: Adjusting strategies and plans creatively in response to changing circumstances. Creative leaders inspire their teams to explore new ideas, embrace change, and pursue continuous improvement, thereby enhancing both individual and organizational performance.

Creativity is the miracle of the Black Church. Innovation, probably not as much. Innovation is all about making something out of nothing. The Black Church was birthed from adversity; it came from the darkness of white supremacy that expelled and excluded Black people, forcing them to create something out of nothing under duress; and it ushered a people into and helped them through Jim Crow and the Civil Rights Movement. The Black Church *is an innovation*. But when one considers the neuroscience research that shows that creativity requires a calm mind in order to focus, that focus is the prerequisite for insight, which is required for creativity, you will know that creativity springing from the Black Church is a miracle in and of itself. How the people of the Black Church get to that calm mind in the midst of historical duress describes the quantum leap, and it smacks of the convergence of the ten positive emotions that both neuroscience and positive psychology research reveal are imperative for success. These ten emotions undergird the science of happiness.

As mentioned earlier, the ten positive emotions, according to psychologist Barbara Fredrickson, are as follows:

1. Love
2. Joy
3. Serenity/Peace
4. Interest
5. Awe

6. Amusement/Fun
7. Pride
8. Gratitude
9. Hope
10. Inspiration

Look again. Many of those positive emotions are the fruits of the Spirit (Galatians 5:22–23). The Bible verse goes on to say that the greatest of these is love; science proves this. Neuroscience research says the most powerful of the positive emotions is love, which is induced by the neurotransmitter oxytocin, which fosters trust as well. The research also shows that it takes at least three concurrent positive emotions to topple a negative mood. All of these positive emotions are engaged simultaneously in the Black Church experience, which unleashes creativity.

These positive emotions are linked to specific brain regions and neurotransmitters, influencing cognitive processes, social interactions, and overall well-being. They engage specific brain regions such as the limbic system, which includes the ventral striatum, amygdala, and orbitofrontal cortex. All of these areas of the brain play a crucial role in experiencing pleasure and reward, which are key components of positive emotions. The left prefrontal cortex, particularly the dorsolateral (where memory happens) and medial regions, is associated with the formation and regulation of positive emotions, along with reductions in activity in the right prefrontal cortex and temporoparietal cortex. The neurotransmitter dopamine and opiate and GABA receptors usher in states of pleasure and contribute to motivation and satisfaction. Other neurotransmitters and hormones like serotonin, endorphins, and oxytocin are also stimulated with these positive emotions and contribute to peaceful and euphoric moods, bonding, and well-being.

The Black Church has been a happy place for generations, spawning creativity and innovation that Black business leaders have taken to work and absorbed into their own success—to the benefit of those they lead. That happiness has led them to optimal creativity, which is more than just a skill—it is a mindset and a strategy. The Black Church's emphasis on creativity, improvisation, and emotional intelligence equips leaders with the ability to engage, adapt, inspire, and innovate. By embracing these principles, leaders can break barriers, drive transformation, and create cultures where bold ideas thrive.

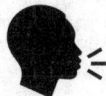

THE LEADERSHIP LESSONS

Creative leaders inspire and engage. Leaders who infuse creativity into their leadership style can energize teams, build engagement, and make lasting cultural impact. Leaders should think beyond traditional methods of communication and engagement, using creative storytelling, interactive experiences, and unique rituals to build stronger connections with their teams.

Improvisation and adaptability are essential leadership skills. The ability to pivot, adjust, and make decisions in real time is crucial for effective leadership, particularly in unpredictable situations. Leaders must develop the skills of reading the room; adjusting strategies based on team dynamics, market shifts, or audience engagement; and knowing when to change course for the greatest effect.

Creativity enhances emotional intelligence and influence. Leaders who are attuned to emotions and understand how to create effective moments foster stronger relationships and greater influence. Leaders should develop emotional intelligence by actively listening, observing reactions, and adjusting their approach to resonate with different audiences.

Risk-taking and confidence fuel innovation. Bold leaders take calculated risks, trust their instincts, and step outside their comfort zones to achieve breakthrough success. Leaders should embrace uncertainty, trust their intuition, and take creative risks that push their organizations forward.

A positive environment unlocks creativity. Creativity flourishes in environments that inspire, uplift, and generate positive emotions, making culture building a critical leadership responsibility. Leaders should intentionally cultivate environments where team members feel safe, valued, and inspired, as this sparks innovation and unlocks their full creative potential.

COACHING QUESTIONS

How do you currently incorporate creativity into your leadership style, and where could you push the boundaries to inspire greater engagement and innovation in your team?

CALL AND RESPONSE

Think of a time when you had to pivot unexpectedly in your career or leadership journey. How did you handle it, and what did you learn about your ability to adapt under pressure?

How can you create an environment where your team feels encouraged to take creative risks, challenge the status quo, and bring bold new ideas forward?

What aspects of your leadership are rooted in tradition, and how can you balance honoring those traditions while also driving innovation and forward-thinking change?

10
ECONOMIC EMPOWERMENT
Building Kingdoms

It's hard to forget the extravagant dinners held on the front lawn of Good Street Missionary Baptist Church, with its beautiful, iconic red brick building with white trim as the backdrop. Just as summertime came, the sunshine played host to the wonderful alfresco meal the women of the church worked tirelessly to pull off. There were no caterers, unless you counted the volunteers as such, and the food was delicious. Women wore their best frocks and the men and boys were always in their finest suits and ties—a beautiful sight to behold.

It was Black joy and prosperity on display: scores of tables on the lawn with white tablecloths gently blowing in the breeze, children running and playing between bites, beautiful floral displays set out by the Garden Club, women in white A-line dresses and skirts. Sometimes they wore white gloves as they distributed plates with "Gospel bird," better known as fried chicken, or fried catfish, collard greens, yams, potatoes with gravy, or maybe macaroni and cheese, baked beans, potato salad and a variety of other salads, and dinner rolls. And oh boy, the desserts, like cakes, pies, cookies, and brownies. These dinners were never complete without sweet tea or red punch. Sure, it could be viewed as diabetes on a plate, but that would be addressed during the health fair a few months later.

I have to say that our pastor Dr. C. A. W. Clark "did the thing" when he had Good Street built in the late 1960s on 3110 Bonnie View Road, with doors opening for services in 1970. It was quite an empowering victory when you consider that it was built and now stands where a major plantation in the region thrived for nearly one hundred years. The old Millermore Mansion, which once housed enslaved people and all the trappings of the slave trade, was built in 1855 on the same ground where Black joy, faith, purpose, and empowerment now reign. It was 1,284 acres of grassy knolls, cotton fields, and farmland, which included the land where my childhood home stands to this day. I still remember the old well that was in the front yard of one of my neighbors' homes. We knew it was old, but we didn't know that the enslaved fetched water there. The Millermore Mansion was dismantled and reassembled at Dallas's Old City Park in 1969, where a Dallas history marker acknowledges it today. Many say that it is haunted. The TV show *Ghost Hunters* even paid a visit, seeking out paranormal activity there. The ghosts were totally excommunicated from the land, though, when that ground was broken and blessed to make way for the home of the very symbol of Black empowerment—what many call the country's original Black megachurch, Good Street Missionary Baptist Church.

Good Street was erected within months of the plantation's removal; the elementary school across the street is the only remaining indication that the plantation stood there. The plantation was named for the slave owner and cotton farmer William Brown Miller. The school and church are just adjacent to the street that has the same plantation name, Millermore. To this day, the church stands tall as one of the most beautiful classic church structures in Dallas, Texas, with its towering off-white church steeple, well-manicured green lawn, and sidewalk that ushers you up steps to the double white doors and into the foyer of the sanctuary. Good Street remains a dream venue for weddings because it was one of the only Black churches in Dallas with a bright red center aisle for the dramatic entrance of the bride. In fact, that was how they celebrated the first worship service in 1970. They had a wedding right in the middle of the service. Appropriate after laying a plantation to rest in that same spot just over a year before. A funeral, then a wedding. A new birth for that church, and for me, as I was born a year later. They paid it off and then burned the mortgage on that building when I was ten years old, in 1981—only eleven years after opening the doors. It wouldn't be the first time leadership burned a mortgage in the church's history.

Their first building was named Good Street in reference to their address on Good Lattimer Road in South Dallas. After that building burned to the ground in the late 1940s, they rebuilt it, then immediately opened a charitable foundation, which would purchase a 332-unit apartment complex, called the Good Haven Apartments. It was a sprawling 20,000-square-foot property, complete with a childcare center to serve the community. The church built and opened a nursery and community center, created the second Black Church–owned credit union in the country, and purchased a seventy-passenger bus and two station wagons and other vehicles to transport congregants and community members. Despite all these investments into the community, they still burned the mortgage on that newly built edifice in ten years. The church's ability to do that was an important symbol—that it was about doing real business, being fiscally responsible on its own so that it could be the rock the community could depend on when in need. That was its second function—to provide for the congregation and the community economically. Its first was to provide spiritual enrichment. That a formidable Black congregation laid its roots down on former plantation soil by raising its own money and establishing the good credit needed to build on that soil only two years after King's assassination, so that it could empower the community while praising and worshipping God, is the very illustration of the Black Church experience in the United States throughout time. Churches like Good Street also stand as a symbol of what can be done when you are a good steward of finances.

Burning the mortgage was something the church could do thanks to events like dinners on the grounds, because they became part of a fundraiser, planned and executed on special days and observances. I clearly remember dinners on the grounds being a part of our Women's Day activities, a creative way to honor the church's women and raise money for the building funds, capital campaigns, college scholarships, community outreach efforts, and more. Black churches back then didn't have the corporate sponsors many of the megachurches have today. It really was bootstrapping, and churches like my own were making their own boots.

Our church wasn't the only church hosting events like this, and sometimes they were much more humble endeavors like cake walks, fish fries, bake sales, musicals, recitals, and most often simply passing the offering plate. Sometimes the plate was passed to help someone raise their rent or mortgage. Fundraising became more sophisticated with time, but this was the primary way the Black Church supported its members and those in the community at large who were in need. All of it speaks to the Black Church's deep history of being a place that helps, and many times church food was one of the ways Black people would get the job done.

The "dinner on the ground" concept started back during times of enslavement, when Sundays were often the only day the enslaved people had for rest. Instead of remaining in white churches where they continued to experience the discrimination and meanness they endured all week, Black people established their own Sunday meetings for worship and communal gatherings that represented freedom for them, even if only for one day out of the week. In much of the South, it was against the law for enslaved people to gather and do anything together, especially practicing religion publicly, so many of these makeshift church services happened on the hush, deep in the woods where no one could find them. After the gathering, according to oral histories collected in Texas, the group would meet by the riverbanks and fry fish. I wonder if the enslaved people on the Millermore plantation sought out a hidden place to worship. They say that if you go down the alley behind Good Street today, there is still evidence of the Millermore graveyard, which has grown over and is barely recognizable.

Eventually, with emancipation, some of the newly freed people managed to raise church buildings on their own, but it became a tradition that the people would bring food that they could contribute to the church on Saturday nights so that the cooking could begin first thing in the morning and dinner could be served immediately following the singing and preaching. The enslaved and eventually freed people called this dinner on the ground, and sometimes they'd bring banjo players and players of other instruments to provide live music during the meal. It's amazing how this tradition is still carried out at many of the smaller Black churches to this day. I remember smelling the food cooking during the worship service, a welcome distraction from some of the more boring parts of the service for a kid like me. While initially the dinner on the ground event was all about fellowship, eventually, the ritual became a reliable venue to raise funds.

Economic Empowerment Means Power to the People

Economic power in our community didn't start in boardrooms or bank accounts—it was born in the pews, in offering plates passed hand to hand, in sermons that spoke life into possibility. The Black Church planted those first seeds for many of us—of stewardship, of enterprise, of building something to leave behind. It was the first entrepreneurial endeavor many of us saw modeled. Our pastors were the first entrepreneurs many of us in the older generations would see in our community. Other businesses sprouted from the church's membership. An entire ecosystem sometimes: grocery stores, insurance companies, dress and hat shops, doctor's offices, dentists, attorneys, shoeshine stands, barber and beauty shops, convenience stores, and so much more. It taught us how to stretch a dollar, how to dream bigger, how to have faith while doing the work. It gave us purpose and a language of legacy and a vision of abundance rooted not in lack, but in love. This was more than survival—it was sacred strategy.

We watched it all unfurl—whether it was raising money for Black students to attend colleges and universities, or launching Black banks and credit unions so that the community could have a better shot at approval for a home or car loan without fear of predatory tactics. Barring the occasional church building fund fiasco or love-offering scandal, Black churches showed us how business was done and empowered us to do it ourselves, for our families and for our own businesses. If you needed to make ends meet to pay a water or a light bill, the church was where you went for that kind of help. People kept their homes, thanks to the Black Church, and that helped build generational wealth in the Black community. The Black Church was a symbol and sustainer of Black independence, and even those who didn't believe or didn't attend knew they could be a part of that.

While there may not be as many fish fries happening at churches, and even Good Street brought its dinners on the ground inside due to the brutal Texas heat, this rich history of empowering the community is echoed in the many programs we see unveiled in today's headlines, for example, the billion-plus-dollar venture between T. D. Jakes Enterprises and Wells Fargo to underwrite housing developments, home loans, financial literacy initiatives, entrepreneurial education, and more for the community. Or perhaps it's in the example of how one church in Dallas, Friendship-West Baptist Church, known for its activist pastor, Dr. Frederick Douglass Haynes III, acquired another historic church's credit union, that belonged to St. John Missionary Baptist Church, where Haynes's aunt was the music minister for years. That federal credit union, the third of its kind in the country owned by a Black Church, was on its last legs before closing in 2016. Haynes rebuilt an even more robust financial institution, renaming it the Faith Cooperative Federal Credit Union, offering what it calls "Liberty Loans." These are low- to no-credit microloans of between $200 and $500 without the predatory interest rates that can saddle poor communities with debt, something that is common in that type of lending.

Black Church initiatives don't have to be a mammoth to teach us lessons, though. Some of us learned simply by seeing the smallest of actions around collection plates.

"My father was a steward that counted money," Executive Leadership Council CEO and former human resources executive Michael Hyter said. "My mother was part of the volunteer group that did global work."

Hyter's upbringing in Ebenezer AME Church reflects the practical lessons in finance, responsibility, and service. His family's roles mirror the church's role in teaching generational accountability and economic ethics.

Empowerment is inextricably tied to purpose. Former chief marketing officer and consultant D. Keith Pigues got his business wings in the Black Church and began his entire consultancy with a focus on empowering people to learn their own purpose.

"I help people get more out of work and life than they ever thought possible," he said.

Keith exemplifies how faith and purpose-informed leadership evolve into economic impact. Through his consultancy and tech ventures, he empowers organizations to measure and enhance their value, echoing the Black Church's call for stewardship and accountability. His trajectory from electrical engineer to four-time CMO and founder aligns directly with themes of strategic growth and innovation for community uplift.

When considering what experts say about empowering people, whether through economics or other means, recall that it is a leadership imperative. It's one thing to inspire the people. It is quite another to put the tools in their hands to build on their own terms for their needs. It is the ultimate investment in the community and a force multiplier.

In a 2025 *Forbes* article by Brent Gleeson on empowerment as a leadership trait, Italo Pignano, founder and CEO of EON Medical + Wellness, was quoted as saying, "Empowerment begins with leaders who understand their true purpose: to serve, uplift, and enable others to reach their full potential." Great business leaders recognize that their success is intricately tied to the growth and achievements of their teams and communities.

Still, for other leaders, observing how the Black Church empowered its congregants and the community in turn inspired empowerment as a leadership skill more broadly. Instead of putting money in the hands of their teams, their currency was training, education, opportunity, a shot—all of it could very well lead to increased income in the future once armed with the skills and/or the opportunity. Former Mavericks CEO and AT&T senior executive Cynt Marshall believes that you need to "turn the people loose." That's her term for equipping them with the right tools and then setting them on a path to success on their own terms. She recalls a time when she was being considered for an officer role at the telecom giant AT&T and a superior, someone who looked like her, had given negative feedback about her style, both as a leader and in terms of her fashion. She was prepared to turn the role down, but she recalls then-CEO Ed Whitacre calling her personally to say that he wanted her to take the role and not change one thing about herself. Those words were the empowerment she needed.

"His words turned me loose . . . and let me be Cynt, and that is the power of leadership," she said. She learned about empowerment in her childhood church; her leadership worldview is so intertwined with what she learned there that she calls leadership a "sacred assignment." She transformed the Dallas Mavericks by creating space for authenticity and expression—the currency that she used to empower her church team. She said every move she made was rooted in scripture, shaped by the church, and infused with joy. She designed workplaces where music played, walls spoke values, and every hand left a mark—literally—on the culture.

"We turned the creatives loose... and it was beautiful," she said.

Her approach was simple but radical: "Listen to the people, learn from the people, love the people."

This is how she empowers her teams.

"I want them to walk into a place where they know that the whole person... is welcomed, nurtured, and we want that to thrive."

The Black Church Unleashes a Washerwoman to Become a Powerful, Wealthy Businesswoman with a Vision

They knew her as Sarah Breedlove at the St. Paul AME Church in St. Louis, the widow with the "half-orphan" child, destitute and needing some help, but they saw more than that as well. The women of that church did everything they could to not only get Breedlove back on her feet but also educate her and her daughter with the life skills they needed to thrive. Before she was a millionaire named Madam C. J. Walker, she was a pew-sitter, a prayer-warrior, and a church choir member. She was a widow with a scalp full of sores and matted hair. The sanctuary of the AME church gave Sarah Breedlove more than salvation—it gave her *a sense of possibility*. She also had a dream.

It was in those wooden pews, dressed in all she had, where she found community and connection—somewhere she could place her trust, having arrived in a very vulnerable state. It was in the sermons that named her *worthy*—not just of heaven, but of healing. And it was in the women's circles, the missionary meetings, and the choir lofts where she saw the hidden labor and overlooked beauty of Black women.

"The church was where she organized, where she cast the vision, where she found her people—and reminded them that they were worthy of more," said her great-great-granddaughter and biographer, A'Lelia Bundles. "She was tithing, teaching, and transforming at the same time."

Walker saw the opportunity to lead in church as well. So when she became Madam C. J. Walker, she didn't build an empire for herself alone—she built it for and with the women of the church, for the ushers with calloused hands, for the choir girls with thinning edges, for the kitchen workers and caretakers who had never seen their names on a paycheck, let alone a business card.

She developed hair care not just as a product, but as a promise. And who did she trust to carry that promise to the world?

Church women.

She gave them formulas, but also financial literacy. She taught them to sell, yes, but also to save. To own homes. To build wealth. They weren't just clients. They became her *sales force*. Her "Walker Agents." Her sisters in both spirit and strategy. These were women who had once passed the plate in church. Now, they passed catalogs, orders, and dreams.

And it came full circle. Because every time a tithe was dropped from hands that had once been bound by economic dependence—now loosed and thriving—another layer of the kingdom was built. This is what happens when the Black Church affirms potential in its people. When a woman is told she is *enough* to lead. When empowerment isn't just preached but *practiced*. Madam Walker didn't just build a brand. She built a movement from the sanctuary out.

The thing about economic empowerment is that it doesn't always begin with cash; sometimes it is simply assistance. Sometimes it comes in the form of someone sewing you a dress so that you can go look for work. Other times, it's providing childcare so that you don't have to worry about how to take care of your child once you land the job. That "hand up" from the church fostered an awakening. Suddenly, she saw her own potential, and she began to see it in others as well. Essentially, she started as Breedlove, the nearly destitute, and became Walker, the hair-care mogul, philanthropist, businesswoman force of nature. Let's be clear, though: All of this happened with the help of empowerment from the people of the Black Church.

"She [Madam Walker] was always involved in the AME church, and her philanthropy extended through it. She didn't just want to make money—she wanted to empower other women to be self-sufficient," Bundles said. "She taught them how to run their own businesses, how to keep their books, and how to own property. She used her success not as a finish line, but as a foundation—to lift others up with her."

Empowerment is equipping, and it is the cornerstone of effective leadership. According to the United Nations, when companies increase employment and leadership opportunities for women, enhanced organizational effectiveness and growth follow; this is a significant benefit to the company as well as to those women. A study by Baira Faulks and colleagues published in *Sustainability* also found that empowering people and teams positively influences innovative work behavior, which in turn provokes sustainable economic performance. These leaders are authoritative, and they are able to guide their teams by example, inspiring progression toward common goals, which is essential for economic empowerment even within organizations.

Top financial executive Carla Harris from Morgan Stanley believes that true leaders don't just direct—they inspire and empower. She emphasizes that leadership is a journey from execution to empowerment, where the role of a leader is to create other leaders by giving away power and creating a powerful leverage. When Harris left Catholic mass to be a part of the choir at the Black church where she enjoyed singing, she wasn't just singing in the junior choir; she was watching an inspiring leadership model in the pastor of that Baptist church.

"I would argue that one of the things I learned was the importance of engagement with your people. Even though the pastor had the most power, and there was a hierarchy, he modeled that the most effective leaders in that church were the ones who engaged with people," she said. "If you are that leader, it is important to engage with your people."

Harris believes that leadership is not about position—it's about presence. The best leaders, she says, are those who reach across the divide of power to meet people where they are. It's about listening, connecting, and inviting others into their own strength. Harris also underscored the importance of authenticity in leadership as a currency of empowerment. She said that bringing your authentic self to the table as a leader builds trust. According to the Global Leadership Network's article about Harris, trust also empowers the people you lead to do their best work. Trust is at the heart of any successful relationship. In Harris's view, empowering others involves not only leveraging their strengths but also fostering an environment where diverse perspectives are valued, leading to innovation and organizational success.

Empowerment Is "Power-With" Not "Power-Over"

Neuroscience research supports Harris and Marshall's approach to leadership, which is authoritative in nature, influencing, a sharing of the power. The discipline calls it the "Power-with" approach as opposed to the "power-over" approach, and it takes us back to the neuroscience of connection. It's about connection over control. Shared vulnerability and mutual support strengthen neural pathways linked to trust, cooperation, and innovation. The Black churches that model this well combine the power of community (in the sense of social cohesion) with the ability to shift power to its congregations and the community. Instead of lording over the people, asking them to give, give, give and them never seeing a return, the most effective Black churches know how to build trust so that the people know that the wealth it builds is wealth that will be put into the membership's hands or that of the community at large, so that the community is empowered to build for itself. Everyone thrives.

According to Amy Makice of the Bloomington Center for Connection, the "power-over" strategies rely on hierarchy and control. This approach fosters micromanagement, overworking people, or competition, which will lead to stress and burnout and—in a church that is supposed to be empowering the people and not tearing it apart—plenty of mistrust.

Humans are wired for connection. When they feel disconnected, there is doubt, distrust. When leaders lead with connection at the center, something nearly holy happens. The brain responds, yes—but so does the heart and soul. We are wired not just to survive but to thrive in relationship. And the most powerful kind of leadership? It doesn't command from a distance. It draws near. It empowers.

In healthy Black churches, we saw this firsthand. Pastors who knew your name. Elders and church mothers who pulled you aside, not to scold, but to shape. They didn't necessarily preach prosperity—they modeled stewardship, mutual support, and economic dignity. The building fund, the scholarship drive, the sister who sold pies to send a child to college—this was grassroots empowerment wrapped in spiritual intention.

Rev. Cokiesha Bailey Robinson, associate dean of mentoring and cross cultural engagement at Grace College, an author, and an ordained minister, offers a soul-stirring definition of stewardship that blends theology, leadership, and deep personal conviction.

"I think stewardship is care of—responsible care of—or care of with integrity. How I treat my husband, Timothy Robinson, is my stewardship of my husband," she said. "How I treat this staff is my stewardship. How my school cares for people of color is their stewardship of us. And how we care for parishioners and those in the pew. How we tithe—or lack thereof—is our stewardship. Stewardship is not just financial."

Science now tells us what the Black Church always knew: Trust heals. Mutuality transforms. When people feel seen, safe, and believed in, their minds open, their hearts steady, and their hands get to work. Co-regulation becomes co-creation.

This is what leaders must reclaim: the sacred act of empowering others through presence, trust, and purpose. Not as a strategy, but as a calling.

What the Black Church Teaches Us About Empowerment That Builds Kingdoms

Long before scholars penned theories and scientists mapped the brain, the Black Church was already living out the sacred truth: When people are empowered, they rise. They build. They lead. They thrive. It wasn't theory—it was tradition. It was testimony. It was the hush in the sanctuary and the hum of the fellowship hall. It was a place where young Black boys and girls were told they could speak, lead, own, and *be*. A place where entire communities pooled resources to send someone to school, launch a business, or buy back the block. What we now call *positive psychology*—this science of happiness, strengths, resilience, and human flourishing—the Black Church has been practicing for generations quietly, faithfully, prophetically. Positive psychology views empowerment as a crucial leadership skill, emphasizing the importance of fostering a sense of agency, autonomy, and competence in team members to unlock their potential and drive positive outcomes. Here are tips and insights that leaders can follow to achieve the same trust and connection as modeled by Black churches that center economic empowerment as a value:

Shine a Light on Strength. Leaders who focus on strengths build self-efficacy and unlock performance. Many pastors are leaning into what they know about their congregations and building connections based on their members' strengths. Since the pews are full of professionals and business owners, they highlight their gifts by centering efforts on curating Black business directories and expos, pointing its members to buy from their fellow congregants, and positioning the church as its very own microeconomic engine. By framing its flock not by our deficits, but by its divine potential and possibilities, the institution generates dollars in the community by simply centering itself as the host and facilitator. There is no credit check. No one looks into whether someone's franchisee taxes are current. Having a nice website isn't even a criterion. It's the "whosoever will" spirit that guides the effort. These leaders see the gold before it's refined. Name what's strong, not just what's wrong, calling forth the excellence already stirring in the people.

Make It Safe to Be Brave. Psychological safety fosters risk-taking, creativity, and resilience. A healthy Black church makes it okay to have dings on your credit or none at all, making room for mistakes while filling out the loan papers despite it all at their credit union. This is more than about missed notes in the choir or a fumbled verse on the mic, although that's where the spirit of psychological safety began for many of us when we were young. It could be about re-entry or a soft landing for someone who is looking for another chance after being imprisoned or in rehab. Pointing people the way toward a new life from one that was fraught with peril on the streets. Never a judgment given, always a hand up with social services provided and always followed by grace and guidance. The Black Church was, for many of us, the first place we learned we could fall and still be loved. Empowerment isn't possible where fear or judgment reigns. Leaders should create rooms where people are safe to try, speak, and stretch without punishment. Where failure is feedback, not a finish line.

Offer Autonomy with Trust. Autonomy increases motivation, engagement, and innovation. Black churches that offer housing developments for communities who may not have the access, or partner with large banks to ensure parishioners have access to the capital it takes to become homeowners, are encouraging autonomy that will lead to more financial literacy and empowerment. This is the way to say, not only does the church trust you to take this opportunity and run with it, it's putting skin in the game with you. Stewardship is taught through real responsibility. Leaders can empower their teams by letting go and "letting them loose." Delegate with intention. Trust is the soil where ownership and excellence grow.

Speak the Language of Growth. A growth mindset transforms how people respond to challenges and setbacks. Whether it is seeing the potential in the community and then having a plantation "big house" removed from former plantation land to replace it with a church, running predatory lenders or seedy motels and the shady characters who frequent them out of a neighborhood, or bringing in respected business owners and national chains into that same neighborhood, it's all about transformation, comebacks, and renewal, even for the soul. Black churches through their economic empowerment initiatives hold space for progress over perfection, and that encourages the community to "press toward the mark," not because anyone had arrived, but because we were *becoming*. Leaders should talk about learning as sacred, celebrating growth like celebrating a win. It's all about making room for people to evolve without shame.

Reap the Fruit of Empowerment. Empowered people are more engaged, creative, and committed. Empowered congregations changed zip codes. They continue to birth movements. They build schools, credit unions, scholarship funds, and businesses. They don't just shout about victory; they put their hard-earned money where their mouths are—they *invest* in it. Empowerment isn't just good for morale—it's strategy. It multiplies talent, deepens commitment, and cultivates cultures where people want to stay and grow.

When you empower people, you don't just build a team. *You build a kingdom.*

THE LEADERSHIP LESSONS

See the Gold Before It's Refined. Don't wait for polish before you praise. Speak to the promise you see, even if it's still in seed form. When leaders recognize and name strengths early, they stir self-belief. And belief? That's the birthplace of brilliance. Leadership whispers: "I see something in you." The empowered answer: "Maybe I can see it too."

Make the Room Safe for Risk. Create spaces where people aren't afraid to fumble. Where ideas can be raw and real. Empowerment only grows in safe soil—where feedback is kind, and failure is framed as a step, not a sentence. People bloom when they're no longer bracing for impact.

Give Away Power Like It's Abundant. Hand over the mic. Delegate with joy. Let your people lead in their own way. Trust is not a gamble—it's a gift. And every time you offer it, you build a culture of ownership, excellence, and pride. Control builds compliance. Trust builds leaders.

Preach Process, Not Perfection. Teach your team that growth is sacred. That learning is the win. Create space for development, celebrate effort, and remind them that transformation isn't just possible—it's expected. The journey is the destination when you believe in becoming.

Build What Outlasts You. Empowerment is a legacy move. When you lift others, you don't just reach the goal—you raise a generation. Empowered teams don't just execute. They elevate. They create. They carry the mission further than you ever could alone. You're not just building a team. You're building a kingdom.

COACHING QUESTIONS

How are you creating space where your people can fall—and still feel held?

What are you building that will bless others long after you're gone? What are you planting today that will grow into shelter, strategy, or sacred opportunity tomorrow?

Do the people you lead feel seen for their gifts—or only measured by their output? How might your leadership affirm the divine potential in your team—even before it's fully polished?

THE INVITATION
A Letter to Leaders

Dear Leader...

This chapter is where the call and response happens for you. It's how I figuratively open the doors of the church for you whether the Black Church was or is a part of your experience or not. This church that I'm inviting you to join is the one that preaches faith and purpose, community, speaking and storytelling, resilience, perseverance, collaboration, accountability, social justice, creativity and innovation, and economic empowerment to raise up more excellent and unflappable leaders into the C-Suites of corporate America, centering intention, social cohesion, self-determination, and wielding positive emotions, all to foster better organizations, better businesses, and the greater good.

This is what many Black preachers do just as they wrap up a sermon and the choir begins to sing right before the benediction is called: they open the doors of the church. You can walk up the aisle, or in some tech-savvy churches, you can simply scan a QR code. Either way, it's an invitation to join. In this case, the invitation is not to salvation, but it *is* to save a leadership pipeline that is not as strong as it used to be. It is an invitation to a new way of thinking about leadership, a new way of approaching it that may have seemed a little antiquated at the onset of this book; however, throughout the pages you realized that this approach is no doubt time-tested and proven through science. It is indeed evidence-based and provides a solid framework for any leader aspiring to be great. Now is the time to explore ways to preserve the leadership pipeline that began so many generations ago from the pews of this cultural institution.

I'll be the first to admit that I almost forgot about the Black Church and how it could play a role in my training as a business leader; however, I attend faithfully, whether online or in person. That over there is about faith, I would say. This over here is business. But as former Dallas Mavericks CEO Cynt Marshall put it, "There's no way to separate a person from their faith walk, especially when it comes to how they show up in leadership and life," adding that her leadership is directly informed by her spiritual beliefs and values—and that authenticity in leadership includes bringing your whole self, including your faith, to the table. She is not wrong. In fact, these guiding principles are embedded in my being, becoming such a routine part of my life that I hadn't given the Black Church the credit due for being the diamond mine that produced this gem of a career that I've had over the years and the gem of a leader that I'm proud to say I've become throughout my life in all aspects of it, but especially in business, whether inside or outside the halls of corporate America.

I listened to many of the leaders lament in our conversations that they never really viewed the Black Church through a professional lens before, an exploratory lens filtered through the focus of neuroscience and positive psychology—fields that leadership experts turn to for proof of concept. These executives never really thought of the Black Church as the first place that made them the polished executives they are today, because it was an extension of home to them. It seemed old-fashioned, maybe even a bit regular—to most, imperfect. As wireless CEO Xavier Williams mentioned, the first memory of the Black Church that came to his mind was that it was a place where everyone just seemed old. So, to consider that it is the place where all of these leaders received their wings to fly and be who they turned out to be, people who frequent corporate and private jets, boardrooms and major platforms . . . it seems miraculous, almost, and has moved some of them to tears.

This imperfect environment that is the Black Church, full of shortcomings like any other organization of faith or otherwise—when it adheres to the core values and methods that brought it thus far through slavery, Reconstruction, Jim Crow, the Civil Rights Movement, and even modern-day strife—is an environment that nurtures and exudes all ten positive emotions at once at any given moment, causing our brains to fire off neurons at the right moments to stir up a neurological amalgam for success. Over time, we've treated it as our filling station, powering us up to go back into a society that week after week shows us every reason we should give up. Yet, we still press on thanks to a divine progress loop kicked off by a sermon, a song, service to the community, or even something within us. How can we continue to not only recognize this wellspring of business talent, but fuel it?

Something's Different These Days

I will admit that this challenge that I'm laying out for you is even more personal than I thought. As I look at my daughter, who is now twelve, I can clearly see that she has missed out on the experiences that I had in leadership when I was her age—experiences that are difficult to come by outside the Black Church. It isn't her fault. She's been right with me in the congregations, attending Sunday School when she was very young at Good Street Baptist Church. She was tiny, but she was at least afforded the opportunity to do an Easter speech before she began attending the larger churches with me. Sunday School existed at one of the churches we attended, but that one-to-one relationship with the teacher was nonexistent because there wasn't just one dedicated teacher there who would get to know the students. That made the experience feel less personal, as if she was just another number, herded along to classrooms, snack time, and then reconvening. No one knew her well enough, and the programs were not built to afford the young congregants the chance to lead anything, barring an occasional reading of a scripture to peers in a small group. By the time she entered fifth and sixth grade, the students were herded into one big room where they had a "children's church," which mimicked the adult version—great for singing along, but still very impersonal. All of the students onstage seemed like they may have had agents, perhaps. They sang like they'd been in a Disney movie. A little intimidating for the kids who hadn't polished their talents yet, and it felt more isolating. The "whosoever will" spirit that I grew up with, for which standing on the platform was actually more an offering or practice than a performance, seems to have faded in many of the larger churches, with smaller churches attempting to emulate the larger ones.

Enter the pandemic, and any chance of personal connection went out of the window for both of us, but it was starker for my daughter because she was at that age—eight and nine years old—when many of us who came through the Black Church had had multiple opportunities to lead. No one has offered her the chance to lead the bus ministry, introduce the guest preacher, lead a solo in church (she did that a couple of times in school), welcome the visitors, or join the junior usher board or hospitality committee, which seems to not exist in many churches these days.

Then there's the technology. Now to be clear, online church has been a blessing to me when I've been on the road and unable to be in the sanctuary. She and I have streamed services at 33,000 feet when Wi-Fi was available or when in a different time zone, or when an ocean away on vacation. Somehow the convenience of it makes it seem like the easy way out sometimes. Granted, when I'm not feeling well, that makes sense, but I questioned it one day when my daughter suggested we stream just because she wanted to sleep a little longer one Sunday morning. I wouldn't have ever dreamed of suggesting missing in-person worship when I was growing up because we simply knew not to say it to our parents. The intergenerational friendships that we fostered at a young age seem all but a thing of the past for my daughter, although she vaguely remembers faces and names from Good Street and the church we attend now because I have held those relationships close. However, there are some relationships she will never be able to foster. At the age of twelve, I had relationships with pastors from all over the country simply because my father gave me the assignment to ensure that the preacher of the day had the lapel mic and that they knew to only turn it on when they entered the sanctuary, and not a moment sooner so we wouldn't catch any untimely banter (or worse—flushes) on the monitors. I mentioned to my friend who pastors one of Dallas's oldest and largest white churches just the other day that I tend to make friends with pastors because of this small job that I did every week.

It's clear that my daughter won't get the leadership lessons I did, but I don't believe it is too late. Adolescence is when most of us become who we will be. Developmentally, our brains are open to these things. Our personalities are taking shape. We are learning more about the world and who we might be in it at that time. What I learned from the executives who said that their "leadership lesson moment" in the Black Church came to them at younger ages was even deeper, however. They described not only the firm nudges and coaching from parents, and the ministry leader putting them out front; they described something inside that drove and motivated them to do it even if their knees were knocking. Some of them knew no fear, like opera legend Denyce Graves who was put in charge of the Sunday School bus ministry when she was only nine years old, or accessibility-tech executive Heather Dowdy who was told to sign ASL impromptu for the congregation when she was twelve, or former Dallas Mavericks CEO Cynt Marshall who stood up to preach when she was fifteen, or CEO of the Executive Leadership Council Michael Hyter who recited a scripture and introduced the preacher for the day atop a wooden box so that he could reach the microphone in the pulpit, or Wall Street executive Carla Harris who slipped into the youth choir at a Baptist Church at thirteen and adheres to every leadership lesson she learned there to this day in boardrooms and conference rooms despite her Catholic upbringing—or even me, when my minister of music put me out front as a soloist with the adult mass choir backing me up or when I was assigned an adult Sunday School class to teach at fourteen. We all knew that this was something we had to do, and we wanted to do it. Not because of what it did for us, but what it did for the ministry, and much more, God's Kingdom.

Where to Go from Here?

If you are mid-career, a C-Suite leader, someone in between, or more junior in rank, you may be wondering what everything uncovered within these pages means for you, especially if you didn't or don't attend church. Even if you did or still do, you may be wondering the same or if you missed something, or if it is too late.

Call and Response is all about a clarion call that I felt deeply moved to make so that leaders like you could respond, but not simply with an *"Amen!"* or a *"Preach!"* like a congregation responding to a Black preacher in the midst of his whoop in a sermon, but with a response to a distinct call to action. That call is simple. It is to consider and then act on the following three areas:

Follow the great example of leadership of the Black Church. You can do that no matter who you are. Consider the ten leadership lessons intentionally and incorporate them into your lives and leadership. Pass them along to those you lead to impact the culture and performance of your organizations and teams. Your leadership and the people you serve will be better for it. It has brought us "a mighty long way."

Reach back into the community with sponsorship for leadership programs that emphasize the ten lessons. I'm working on a curriculum now, based on this book, to share with church leaders and corporate leaders, but until that is ready to go, select one lesson and ask yourself how to join forces with a Black Church leader to move the needle in that one area, buttressing that talent fountain from the pews to the leadership pipeline.

Collaborate with Black churches or one of the many nonprofits that are key partners within their orbit and that take transformational insights and resources to their followers that will strengthen the potential for more leadership lessons. This call is especially for those executive leaders who continue to be affiliated with the Black Church. You are the glue. You know what was and what could be. You know that while it may be impractical to go backward, you know how to drive the innovation and push forward with what we now have in hand—more sophisticated technology, young people who want to be more engaged in social justice and community engagement, church leaders who see the dire need to hang on to the younger generation and meet their needs where they are.

This is why I must turn my attention to Black Church leaders for a moment.

What to Do When the Pews Aren't Overflowing with Young Adults

As I explored all the reasons why the younger generations have been leaving church, Black or otherwise, millennial Donnell McLachlan, also known as the TikTok Theologian, confirmed for me what I knew in my soul might be true. It is likely wishful thinking to assume that if the Black Church pulls the right levers, those who have left will come back.

"The church can't just expect the younger generation to come back. That assumes they were fully there in the first place. We've got to meet them where they are—online, in conversation, in authenticity—not just in pews."

In his opinion, the Black Church doesn't understand the internet, and that is where the conversations that take up the bulk of young people's mindshare take place. He agreed that while many churches have a presence on social media and some on podcasts, the way Gen Z and younger millennials tend to consume their information, they haven't quite learned how to engage, and he wonders if they even care to. A quick survey of many of the Black churches that are online reveals that they've become pretty good at publishing, some even have their own podcasts, but it is a one-way conversation, mirroring the way McLachlan says it's been for generations in the Black Church: It talks at you, but rarely does it listen or encourage young people to talk about the issues that they are actually dealing with.

"The Black Church, in my opinion, fails miserably when it comes to podcasting and social media. And that's where Gen Z lives," he said. "That's where the younger millennials live. They want to hear something that speaks to them in their world, not just on Sunday morning in a sanctuary. So, when we say we want them back, are we actually showing up where they already are?"

To be fair, before deciding against a career in ministry and leaving the church altogether, McLachlan's experience in the Black Church was, on the whole, much like many of the leaders in this book, and very similar to Cynt Marshall's. He grew up in the Pentecostal tradition and did every job there was to do in ministry from preaching to teaching Sunday School, singing in the choir, directing plays, and even doing occasional janitorial duties, all as a teen until he left his small church and became involved in a nondenominational church that didn't feel so stringent. But it still wasn't welcoming questions. Then he headed to college. That's where he experienced a place where he could ask the questions he felt weren't welcomed in the church he described as based in "purity culture, fear-based and fire and brimstone." College is where he was first introduced to theology class. Questioning the faith was accepted there, expected.

However, when I asked him about the leadership lessons he learned in the Black Church, his countenance changed. He saw his pastor as a role model because he said that he knew how to "show up," and that is the one thing that the Black Church taught him that he still uses in his life today, personally and professionally. He will always show up.

"The pastor that I came up under, he showed up, like he showed up to his space. He made sure to keep the grounds. This is something that he committed his life to," he reflected. "And this is one of the first examples of me seeing somebody being the leader and not just, I'm here to talk to y'all on Sundays, but I'm here during the week cleaning up. I'm here, you know, trying to do things, making sure the budget is good.

"He consistently showed up to make sure everything was good. And that lesson in leadership was invaluable because that consistency is what helps us to get to where we're trying to go. You can't just half step when you're doing something. So, lessons in loyalty, lessons in commitment, lessons in discipline. This is my discipline. I'm committed to this, to this work, and to these people, and to this building, to these grounds. So, I think that is probably the most valuable lesson that I learned."

CALL AND RESPONSE

Seeing the Opportunity

Perhaps this is our moment to show up. The moment to open the dialogue between corporate leaders and church leaders, between young people and elders: How can the Black Church reclaim its positioning as "The Original B-School"? Is there an opportunity to leverage technology in a way that doesn't isolate us in our homes, but brings us together over the issues that really matter to our future leaders? And what opportunities can we provide to them to step up into "grown folk's" shoes and lead the way today's top Black leaders remember it happened for them? It won't look the same, and we shouldn't expect it to; however, the outcomes should be the same. We need more C-Suite leaders like Trudy Bourgeois, who advises the top levels in corporate leadership with a keen sense of empathy. Or like D. Keith Pigues, guiding leaders and organizations on the pathway to clarity of purpose; like Adrion Porter, using his speaking ability to show executives how they can master mid-career and mid-life times; like Carla Harris, who's taking the financial world and the gospel music world by storm; like Cynt Marshall, who transforms organizations by loving and empowering the people; like Xavier Williams, whose suave presence and persuasion and business acumen has won him multiple top seats at companies; like Heather Dowdy, who now develops technology that empowers access for people with different abilities for some of the biggest tech companies on the planet; like the four Black candidates for US president on major tickets who showed us how to make history while running for and in one case claiming the highest leadership post in the land; like Denyce Graves, who became "The World's Favorite Carmen" as an opera singer and now empowers young artists with access and training to more opportunities through her business and foundation; like Renee Horne, who now sits atop one of the world's largest financial institutions as one of their chief marketers; like Madam C. J. Walker, who built her multimillion-dollar, self-made empire from her ability to empower other women; or like me, who made an impact in the corporate world, but is now writing leadership books that boldly delve into cultural issues with the power of science to create a force multiplier, producing more strong leaders for change. The Black Church birthed all of us. Now, it's up to us to reignite this leadership engine that is primed and ready to produce more.

THE COACHING GUIDE

Thirty-Eight Powerful Questions Based on the Ten Lessons to Usher You to Extraordinary Leadership

To leverage this guide as a coaching tool, follow this approach as you work through the questions: **Think** about the answer to the question. **Say** your answer out loud for clarity and more insight. **Write** your answer down. **Share** your thoughts with a mentor or coach so that you can map out a strategy. Mindfulness moments like these will ignite breakthroughs as you make your way to higher levels of leadership.

LEADERSHIP LESSON #1
Faith and Purpose

Where did you first uncover your sense of purpose, and how can you engage it to lead others in business as you aspire for the next level?

What can you learn from the childhood experiences of these leaders in the Black Church, and how can you apply it to your own leadership quest in your life today?

How can you build your empathetic leader muscle in the work that you do today for better impact?

If you are struggling with a sense of purpose, take some time to outline the things that you value and let that guide you. List at least three big concepts or ideas that drive or motivate you.

Recount a transformative story from your childhood, whether in the Black Church or not, that shapes who you are as a leader today.

LEADERSHIP LESSON #2
Community

What can you do beginning today to intentionally create connections inside of work and outside of work to create powerful, purposeful relationships?

What can the community-building traditions in the Black Church teach us about navigating the hierarchies within corporate and other business entities?

At what point do you feel most isolated in the workplace, and what best practices from the Black Church can you engage to begin to build connections?

What communities do you tap into when you need a boost of happiness to get you through a challenging time at work? How can you foster deeper connections?

LEADERSHIP LESSON #3
Speaking

What can you take away from the Black preacher in your quest to become a better speaker?

How might you approach storytelling differently after reading about the Black Church tradition?

What might you do to integrate more performance into your leadership in order to benefit from happiness triggers?

What best practices in speaking, storytelling, or performance can you glean from the Black Church that might affect the next generation of Black leaders?

LEADERSHIP LESSON #4
Resilience

What are the major lessons from a Black leader's experience with building resilience in the Black Church?

What obstacles have you faced that could have benefited from better resilience in you?

How will you intentionally cultivate resilience as you aspire for better leadership?

Who in your life demonstrates resilience or grit? What is their story? How do you believe they built it?

LEADERSHIP LESSON #5
Perseverance

The last time you faced adversity, uncertainty, or a steep challenge, how did you respond?

How can you engage hope and anticipation to stoke determination and perseverance in the people you lead?

When was the last time you felt hopeless? If you were to face an equally adverse challenge, how might you approach it knowing what you now know about the power of perseverance?

LEADERSHIP LESSON #6
Collaboration

What leadership lessons can you take from Black Church choirs and music ministries to apply to and improve on your work and your business or corporate America?

Now that your team must bond in order to perform at its peak, what will you do to foster team building and community building within your organization?

What can a Black Church choir teach us about people who have differences working together for a common goal, and how can you apply that to your leadership journey?

LEADERSHIP LESSON #7
Accountability

How do you currently hold yourself accountable in your leadership role, and where might you need to strengthen that accountability?

Think of a time when you had to balance personal responsibility with the needs of a team or organization. How did you navigate that challenge, and what did you learn from the experience?

Who are the mentors, colleagues, or team members who help keep you accountable? How can you cultivate a culture of shared accountability within your organization?

Reflecting on the intrinsic motivation that drives you, how can you better align your personal values with the way you lead and hold yourself accountable?

LEADERSHIP LESSON #8
Social Justice

How does your leadership reflect a commitment to justice and equity, and in what ways could you take a stronger stand on issues that affect marginalized communities?

Think of a time when you witnessed or experienced injustice in your workplace or community. How did you respond, and what might you do differently next time to be a more effective advocate?

The prophetic voice in the Black Church has long been a source of courage and truth-telling, and it rewires our brains for bravery. How can you incorporate boldness and integrity in your leadership while balancing the realities of corporate or institutional constraints?

What steps can you take to ensure that the next generation of leaders—especially those from underrepresented backgrounds—is empowered to use their voices for the values about which they are passionate?

LEADERSHIP LESSON #9
Creativity and Innovation

How do you currently incorporate creativity into your leadership style, and where could you push the boundaries to inspire greater engagement and innovation in your team?

Think of a time when you had to pivot unexpectedly in your career or leadership journey. How did you handle it, and what did you learn about your ability to adapt under pressure?

How can you create an environment where your team feels encouraged to take creative risks, challenge the status quo, and bring bold new ideas forward?

What aspects of your leadership are rooted in tradition, and how can you balance honoring those traditions while also driving innovation and forward-thinking change?

LEADERSHIP LESSON #10
Economic Empowerment

How are you creating space where your people can fall—and still feel held?

What are you building that will bless others long after you're gone? What are you planting today that will grow into shelter, strategy, or sacred opportunity tomorrow?

Do the people you lead feel seen for their gifts—or only measured by their output? How might your leadership affirm the divine potential in your team—even before it's fully polished?

Acknowledgments

Each time I've written acknowledgments, I've done them the way you do when you stand before the Black Church to speak: giving honor to God, the pastor, leaders on the rostrum, family, and friends. Seems like that is not only the right order to offer thanks, but also is appropriate for this particular book. So, I thank God for giving me the wisdom, insight, resources, and references to write this book. It has been a true labor for leadership and love, and He has been overseeing this work. I've simply been a vessel.

As you may have picked up, in the midst of writing this book, my home church changed. I'm back where I belong, under the leadership of Rev. Bryan L. Carter, who as of late has made me so very proud as he has lifted his prophetic voice in ways that our people need direly, centering liberation theology with some good, solid, Word-centered expository preaching . . . and you can always count on the call and response at the end. Pastor Carter truly holds up the light of the Black Church, and writing this book helped me find my way back to Concord Church in Dallas. It also helped me find my way back home in so many other ways too.

Revisiting the history of the Good Street Baptist Church uncovered a startling moment in time, learning that my childhood

ACKNOWLEDGMENTS

home, which was not even a half mile away, sat on the same plantation soil as the church. All the fond memories of growing up in that church are peppered throughout this book. And while so many of the church mothers and elders have since passed away, including Pastor C. A. W. Clark, who left us in 2008, it was great to reach out to my contemporaries, dear friends who grew up there with me, and share parts of the book and outtakes to reminisce, laugh, and even get some facts corrected by them. All of that went into making this book what it is today. The storytelling makes this leadership book leap off the shelf, and for that, I'm thankful to Good Street for being such a rich part of my life and a rich part of the Dallas community and the nation at large.

As always, I have to thank my family. It isn't often that authors get to count family among their most rabid fans, but let me tell you, between my mother, Media Smith, and all three of her sisters, Jackie Ford, Mable Powell, Sapora Radford, I stay hyped up, online and off. As a fan of Marvel movies, I like to call them the Mama Variants. All of them read my books, some of them in one sitting; at least two of them are fans of *The Culture Soup Podcast*®, and at the last family gathering that I couldn't attend recently, my aunties knew more about my speaking schedule than my sister did.

To my father, James E. Smith, I give so much thanks. He's quiet, but he is my loudest fan because of his actions. He and my mother have been a rock for me and my daughter, Joni, especially as business got bumpy with dried-up corporate budgets for the heritage months when I make most of my speaking appearances. Neuroscience says you must have a calm mind in order to focus, so that you can gain insight to be creative. My parents' being there when revenue was scarce for a few months helped me to regain my calm mind and focus so that I could write this book.

ACKNOWLEDGMENTS

So many of the stories that I tell, about the people and pastors I had access to growing up, were possible because my father had me doing assignments around the church. Some of the church folk criticized him for giving me work that "wasn't what a little girl should be doing." He didn't believe in all that. Ensuring the lapel mic made it downstairs and onto the pastor and guest preachers was only part of the job. That wasn't the part that got stuck in the critics' craw. Daddy taught me how to run the board of the church sound system as well, and I was just thirteen.

Daddy lost both his brothers while I was writing this book. His big brothers were twins. Homer and Harvey Smith passed on within months of each other. It was hard for him and all of the family, but Daddy was still encouraging me to write this book despite it all.

Now to my daughter, Joni, only twelve as I write this. Joni is special. She loves her mama, but sometimes she gets really bored listening to audio or watching videos of her mommy talk. Let's face it, TV and radio interviews have been happening to her mommy since she was four, so it all seems pretty regular to her. But the day I learned that this book would be published by a Big 5 publisher with the help of EGOT Viola Davis and her husband, Julius Tennon, was the day I won my baby's attention back because she was like, "Whhhaaaaaaat?!" Don't get me wrong, she is proud of her mommy, and she is my biggest fan (and it's tough to eclipse my mother in that area), but right now, she is proud of her mommy for just being Mommy. All that other stuff will come when we deplane in some far-flung place and she sees my book in the airport bookstore. I'm just glad that she provides me with the chance to have the greatest title of all—mother. It's an honor, and I'm so proud of the beautiful, smart, and sharp-witted young lady that she is becoming.

Now, to the day-one, the original bestie, the ride-or-die even

ACKNOWLEDGMENTS

when we got on each other's nerves when we were little, the PhD of the family, my big sister "Joycie," as I proudly still call her today—thank you! Talk about someone who is right there through thick and thin. She and I have become partners who tag-team through life's biggest curveballs. It helps that she and my brother-in-love, Johnson, only live moments away from my doorstep. She fills in as VP Mommy for Joni when I have business to tend to, and even attends volleyball games and other sporting events that my daughter participates in. She's also joined the pickup and drop-off ministry. Dr. C. Joyce Price helps me keep my sanity and also tag-teams on senior support duties as my parents matriculate to emeritus status in life. These doctor visits tend to multiply with age, and we never have conflict over whose turn it is to take the folks to their appointments, and we work well together on all the other things that life and even the deaths of their siblings or other close family can bring. Thank you, Dr. Auntie Joycie. You're a great sister, and that has helped me complete this book.

I have to thank my brother-in-love, Johnson Price, who has been the keeper of my image since 2002 and is the photographer responsible for my image on this book. He helped me do my big one, and he holds my sister down and cheers for me. Thank you!

I have a slew of cousins, but only the offspring of my mother's eldest brother, who has long since passed away, have been right there with me through the release of *Yes Please! 7 Ways to Say I'm Entitled to the C-Suite* and *Call and Response*, and in ways I couldn't have anticipated. Leon and Yolanda Turner, Anita and Travis Evans, and "my girls," your girls, 'Nita, Joycelyn, Jackie, and even Jessica—thank you for being extended nuclear family to me, Joni, and the rest of my family. These are the cousins that not only show up to book signings and tell people about your books but drive miles to show

ACKNOWLEDGMENTS

up to the funeral of family on the other side of the family tree—then jump in as pallbearers. I don't even need to mention all the wonderful gatherings where we play card games, solve all the world's ills, discuss church chatter, laugh, and cry together—or when I load up the car with Joni, Jackie, Joycelyn, and Jessica, or some variation of that crew, and explore museums, restaurants, movies, and malls together. You've been a treasure trove of positive emotion, especially love, joy, and fun for me while writing this book, and I thank you.

My friends are die-hard, and what's awesome is they aren't here in Dallas with me. Eva Greene Wilson, you and I are so thick, Siri and Google Docs auto-complete your name, like it did just now when I wrote this. The technology knows, which is a little scary, but who am I hiding it from? Your sweet family has become my own, even if we don't see each other as often as we'd like, but I have to call out your sweet husband, Don, and the adult kiddos Eden, Dave, and Evan—all geniuses in their own right, and some of the kindest human beings you could meet, always engaging online with hearts and cheers. I'm so proud of them and can't wait to meet the twins, your latest begets—the grands! I will never forget calling you guys while you were on the road and sharing the news about this book. Don had to pull over and went immediately into a praise break. You two and your kids laugh and cry with me, and my win was your win. That's family.

Since we're in DC with the friend roll call, I can't forget you, Randy Brown. We go a long way back, but as of a few years ago when we intentionally reconnected, you really have been a sounding board both in business and in life, and sometimes I wonder, "Who's the life coach on this call, really?" because you've got enough insight and powerful questions to last for days. You and your brother Russell show up for me when it counts, and I appreciate you both.

ACKNOWLEDGMENTS

You have been cheering my practice and my books on for some time now, and it means so much. Your mama and daddy, Lorenzo and Jamie Brown, did a good thing when they brought you two into the world and raised you, and I am grateful they became a part of my life back in 2002 so that I could write this today.

Michael Lehman, you stepped in and made the deal happen, and you have been "waiting in the cut" a while to do that at the behest of our friend Joseph "Rev Run" Simmons. Our relationship spans back to 2015 and the work we were doing together for the big company. Throughout that time, we became good friends, and you are still making deals on my behalf, and I thank you for that. I appreciate you more than you know, and I look forward to more worthwhile projects that we will work on together for the greater good. Rev, if you're reading, thank you to you and Justine and the rest of the Simmons family who have been a quiet part of my journey, including Vanessa and Uncle Perry. They are always cheering from afar, and I'm grateful!

To Dr. Henry Louis Gates Jr., who responds to my emails lightning fast with a "Hi, Friend!" every time—you always come through in more ways than one. I won't forget the time that I wanted to finally get some answers about whether I was related to a well-known celebrity that you had on your show who shares the same surname with a branch in my family tree. You didn't just share the public information you had; you connected me to your genealogists! Well, I still don't know because I haven't been able to dig into it as much as I have wanted to, but everything I need is there when it's time to prove it once and for all. You've been supportive and cheering for me openly since the day we met over the phone in 2017, and your contribution to this book is so valued. The sheer weight of your name in association with this book is priceless, and I thank you. I

ACKNOWLEDGMENTS

still plan to take you up on the offer to visit your classroom at Harvard whenever you're teaching, so look out for that soon.

A'Lelia Bundles, I have no words. That the direct descendant of the first woman self-made millionaire in the United States is someone I call friend, and she calls me friend back, is just bonkers to me. Thank you for supporting me from the first day with my PR agency back in the day, to being on my show three times to discuss your projects, to interviewing *me* at my own DC book signing back in 2023. Offering me the nugget about Madam Walker and the AME church was sheer gold to this book, and I will never forget it.

There are so many other people that I need and want to thank, but I don't have all the room: Thank you to the Executive Leadership Council (ELC), which not only provided plenty of platforms for me to speak and facilitate but also allowed me to tap into their fellows to do the research that fueled this book and the one before it. Finally, thank you to their president, Mike Hyter, and participating members of ELC and all the other leaders who lent their voice to this first-of-its-kind book. It is a multiplier, and I can't wait to see the lives and leaders who are transformed because of it.

We had our moment in time to take a moon shot at changing the world by way of the business bookshelf with *Call and Response*, and we did it. I can't wait to see the ripple effect.

I thank you all.

Resources

CALL-AND-RESPONSE CHURCHES

Good Street Baptist Church—*Dallas, Texas*
The author's first church home, where she worshipped for more than twenty-five years. A foundational church shaping young Black leaders, where public speaking and leadership were instilled from childhood.

Concord Church—*Dallas, Texas*
The author's current church of more than twenty years, shaping young leaders, adapting to modern shifts in church culture. It was founded by Rev. Cokiesha Bailey Robinson's father, Rev. E. K. Bailey.

Apostolic Faith Church—*Chicago, Illinois*
Accessibility tech leader Heather Dowdy first translated American Sign Language here at the age of twelve.

Ebenezer AME Church—*Detroit, Michigan*
CEO of the Executive Leadership Council Mike Hyter's childhood church, where faith, leadership, and service were a way of life.

RESOURCES

Union Missionary Baptist Church—*Lansing, Michigan*
The church Hyter attended while in college.

New Macedonia Baptist Church—*Memphis, Tennessee*
Founder of Mid-Career Mastery and speaker Adrion Porter's childhood church, a small but mighty sanctuary where early discipline and faith were nurtured.

Boulevard Church of Christ—*Memphis, Tennessee*
The church where Porter was baptized, a defining moment in his faith journey.

Cumming Street Missionary Baptist Church—*Memphis, Tennessee*
Porter's spiritual home during his teenage years, where he grew in faith and community.

Pleasant Grove Baptist Church—*Memphis, Tennessee*
Porter shuttled between Pleasant Grove and New Macedonia when he was younger.

Mother Bethel AME Church—*Philadelphia, Pennsylvania*
The birthplace of the AME denomination, a historic institution of Black faith and activism.

New Sunny Mount Missionary Baptist Church—*St. Louis, Missouri*
As a child, Renee Horne, chief marketing officer of a major financial institution, attended this church, where perseverance and faith are central.

RESOURCES

Mississippi Boulevard Christian Church—*Memphis, Tennessee*
A megachurch known for its strong community impact, and where Horne worshipped.

Mount Olivet Baptist Church—*St. Paul, Minnesota*
A church where Hyter and his family were deeply involved during his time in Minneapolis.

Eagles Nest Church—*Alpharetta, Georgia*
Porter's current church, where he continues to grow in faith and leadership.

Faith Church of God and Son (now Faith Bible Church)—*Washington, DC*
Opera legend and businesswoman Denyce Graves's home church, where she ran the Sunday School bus ministry at nine years old and first found her voice in the choir, learning discipline, collaboration, and confidence.

St. Paul AME Church—*St. Louis, Missouri*
This historic AME church was the spiritual home of Sarah Breedlove and her daughter, A'Lelia Walker. Breedlove later became Madam C. J. Walker after launching her hair-care business. Walker is the great-great-grandmother of author, biographer, and award-winning journalist A'Lelia Bundles.

Shorter Community AME Church—*Denver, Colorado*
The AME tradition provided community and business support to the great-great-grandmother of A'Lelia Bundles at this church.

RESOURCES

Madam Walker was the first woman self-made millionaire in the United States.

Brooklyn Union Baptist Church—*Washington, DC*
This was former AT&T executive and CEO of NWS Xavier Williams's family's spiritual anchor across generations in DC, a place of mentorship and leadership.

Shiloh Church—*Jacksonville, Florida*
Award-winning songwriter and worship minister David Frazier is currently serving as music pastor, shaping worship and inspiring leadership.

Bible Way Church—*Brooklyn, New York*
Frazier's first church home, where he began singing and learned early discipline and confidence.

LOV Nation Church—*Hurst, Texas*
Founded by Tina Williams, wife of Xavier Williams. His entire family was active here for many years.

St. Pius V Catholic Church—*Jacksonville, Florida*
Morgan Stanley senior executive Carla Harris's childhood Catholic church. She attended mass faithfully and was baptized here at three months old.

St. Paul Missionary Baptist Church—*Jacksonville, Florida*
Harris joined the junior choir here from eighth to twelfth grade. Although she is Catholic, this was where she first led and gained leadership skills in the Black Church context.

St. Charles Borromeo Catholic Church—*Harlem, New York*

Harris's current church. She calls it a "Bap-Catholic" church because of its powerful gospel choir, the Gospelites, within the Catholic mass structure.

New Bethel Apostolic Holy Church—*Richmond, California*

Former AT&T executive and retired CEO of the Dallas Mavericks Cynt Marshall's childhood Pentecostal church. She led sermons, coordinated choir, and learned accountability and preparation.

St. Ignatius Catholic Church—*Mobile, Alabama*

The first Catholic church Trudy Bourgeois's family attended during segregation. A foundational place for spiritual discipline and identity.

Christian Union Missionary Baptist Church (next to grandparents' home)—*Mobile, Alabama*

Trudy Bourgeois's grandfather became a deacon here. She sang and read scriptures as a child. It was a safe, empowering environment that nurtured her confidence and voice.

Evansdale United Methodist Church—*Wilson, North Carolina*

This was former chief marketer and consultant D. Keith Pigues's childhood church. He described it as a small, close-knit community where he first experienced belonging, consistent expectations, and early leadership through public speaking. It was here he gave his first Easter speech and was invited into leadership roles even as a child.

Union Baptist Church—*Durham, North Carolina*

As an adult, Keith Pigues served at this church, where he remained actively involved in leadership and ministry. He referenced it as a church where he was formed, where "Black excellence" was modeled from the pulpit to the congregation, and where he learned to "stand on the shoulders of others."

HISTORICALLY SIGNIFICANT BLACK ORGANIZATIONS INVOLVED WITH THE BLACK CHURCH

For those who are interested in tapping into the ecosystem for social justice that is organically tied to the Black Church, but not interested in attending worship services, here is a list of non-faith-based organizations that are historically networked with the Black Church and tend to get big things done the analog way, because social cohesion happens offline and you don't have to sing a hymn in a sanctuary to connect with the Black Church and its activism.

Historically and currently, several prominent Black organizations have collaborated with the Black Church in activism, advocacy, and social justice movements. These organizations have worked alongside Black churches to advance civil rights, economic empowerment, education, and community development. Below is a list of some of the most influential groups:

Southern Christian Leadership Conference (SCLC)
Founded in 1957 by Dr. Martin Luther King Jr. and other Black clergy, the SCLC played a pivotal role in the Civil Rights Movement, using the Black Church as its foundation for nonviolent protests and social change. **Website:** nationalsclc.org

Congress of Racial Equality (CORE)
Established in 1942, CORE played a vital role in the Civil Rights Movement, often working with Black churches to organize Freedom Rides and voter registration drives. **Website:** core-online.org

National Association for the Advancement of Colored People (NAACP)
While not a religious organization, the NAACP worked closely with Black churches to challenge segregation laws, support legal cases, and promote social justice. **Website:** naacp.org

CONTEMPORARY BLACK ORGANIZATIONS INVOLVED WITH THE BLACK CHURCH:

National Black Church Initiative (NBCI)
A coalition of 150,000 Black churches focusing on social justice, health, and economic empowerment. **Website:** naltblackchurch.com

Samuel DeWitt Proctor Conference
A national network of African American faith leaders committed to social justice, economic justice, and civil rights. **Website:** sdpconference.info

Black Church PAC
Founded in 2017 to mobilize Black faith leaders and churches in voter engagement, political advocacy, and policy change. **Website:** blackchurchpac.org

RESOURCES

Faith in Action (Formerly PICO National Network)
A faith-based community-organizing network that partners with Black churches on justice issues, including criminal justice reform and racial equity. **Website:** faithinaction.org

National Action Network (NAN)
Founded by Rev. Al Sharpton, NAN collaborates with Black churches on civil rights activism, criminal justice reform, and voting rights advocacy. **Website:** nationalactionnetwork.net

Black Clergy of Philadelphia and Vicinity
An organization of Black pastors and religious leaders in Pennsylvania advocating for racial and economic justice. **Website:** blackclergyphilly.org

The King Center
Established by Coretta Scott King, the center continues the work of Dr. Martin Luther King Jr., working with churches on leadership training, education, and activism. **Website:** thekingcenter.org

The Poor People's Campaign
Revived by Rev. William Barber II, this movement builds on Dr. King's final campaign for economic justice, often working through Black churches. **Website:** poorpeoplescampaign.org

Black Church Center for Justice and Equality
A newer organization dedicated to uniting faith leaders for justice, economic equity, and human rights. **Website:** theblackchurch.net

RESOURCES

HISTORICALLY SIGNIFICANT BLACK CHURCH CONVENTIONS AND DENOMINATIONS

For those looking for Black-church-affiliated groups or a church home where you can get a word in the prophetic tradition and liberation theology while enjoying a choir that doesn't mind throwing in some Walter Hawkins or even an "Old 100," the list below includes church conventions and organizations that were at the center of the fight in the 1950s and '60s and are still actively fighting and having old-school worship today:

National Baptist Convention, USA (NBCUSA)
One of the largest Black religious denominations, NBCUSA had a complex relationship with civil rights activism. Some leaders supported Dr. King, while others were more conservative in their approach. **Website:** nationalbaptist.com

Progressive National Baptist Convention (PNBC)
Formed in 1961 as a breakaway group from the NBCUSA to fully support the Civil Rights Movement and Dr. King's activism. **Website:** pnbc.org

African Methodist Episcopal Church (AME)
The oldest independent Black denomination in the United States, the AME Church has been involved in civil rights activism since its founding in 1816, supporting abolition, voting rights, and modern racial justice efforts. **Website:** ame-church.com

Church of God in Christ (COGIC)

The largest Pentecostal denomination in the US, COGIC was founded in 1907 and is rooted in holiness and charismatic worship traditions. Known for producing strong preachers, musicians, and community leaders, it has long played a central role in Black spiritual life. While not historically as publicly involved in civil rights as Baptist denominations, many COGIC pastors and members were active in the movement and continue to support community development and social justice. **Website:** cogic.org

Bibliography

Preface

Cox, Sherman Haywood, II. "The Whoop in Black Preaching." *Sould Preaching*, September 1, 2019. https://soulpreaching.com/an-introduction-to-the-whoop.

MasterClass. "What Is Call and Response in Music?" Updated August 26, 2021. https://www.masterclass.com/articles/what-is-call-and-response-in-music.

Introduction

Dearmore, Kelly. "Looking Back on When Martin Luther King Jr. Came to Dallas." *Dallas Observer*, January 15, 2024. www.dallasobserver.com/news/looking-back-on-when-martin-luther-king-jr-came-to-dallas-18356719.

Gates, Henry Louis, Jr. *The Black Church: This Is Our Story, This Is Our Song*. Penguin Press, 2021.

Mohamed, Besheer, Kiana Cox, Jeff Diamant, and Claire Gecewicz. "Faith Among Black Americans." Pew Research Center. February 16, 2021. https://www.pewresearch.org/religion/2021/02/16/faith-among-black-americans/.

1: Faith and Purpose—*A Child Will Lead Them*

Goleman, Daniel. "How Purpose and Emotional Intelligence Connect." Korn Ferry, January 5, 2020. www.kornferry.com/insights/this-week-in-leadership/purpose-emotional-intelligence-connection.

Hope, Meredith O., Robert Joseph Taylor, Ann W. Nguyen, and Linda M. Chatters. "Church Support Among African American and Black Caribbean Adolescents." *Journal of Child and Family Studies* 28, no. 11 (2019): 3037–50. www.ncbi.nlm.nih.gov/pmc/articles/PMC7500483/.

Robinson, JoAnn L., Robert N. Emde, and Robin P. Corley. "Dispositional Cheerfulness: Early Genetic and Environmental Influences." In *Infancy to Early Childhood: Genetic and Environmental Influences on Developmental Change*, edited by Robert N. Emde and John K. Hewitt. Oxford University Press, 2001.

Rothbart, Mary K., Stephan A. Ahadi, and Karen L. Hershey. "Temperament and Social Behavior in Childhood." *Merrill-Palmer Quarterly* 40, no. 1 (1994): 21–39.

Whitbourne, Susan Krauss. "What Gives Life Purpose?" *Psychology Today*, June 16, 2023. https://www.psychologytoday.com/us/blog/fulfillment-at-any-age/202305/what-gives-your-life-a-sense-of-purpose.

2: Community—*The Covenant and Circle Unbroken*

Contreras, Russel. "American Churches Remain Largely Segregated—With One Exception." *Axios*, May 18, 2023. https://www.axios.com/2023/05/18/religion-protestant-evangelical-hispanic-latino.

McRoberts, Omar. "Black Churches, Community, and Development." *Shelterforce*, January–February 2001. https://shelterforce.org/2001/01/01/black-churches-community-and-development.

Sharp, Brian. "To Rebuild City Neighborhoods, More Black Churches Are Becoming Developers." WXXI News, November 18, 2024. www.wxxinews.org/local-news/2024-11-18/to-rebuild-city-neighborhoods-more-black-churches-are-becoming-developers.

University of Southern California. "Why Activism Thrives in L.A.'s Black Churches." *USCToday*, February 7, 2022. https://today.usc.edu/black-church-change-social-justice-activism-usc/.

3: Speaking—*The Power of Storytelling and Performance*

Gillian, Deanna. "Spotlight on Confidence: The Science Behind Stage Presence." *Playcrafter Kids Blog*, November 8. https://www.playcrafterkids.com/blog/spotlight-on-confidence-the-science-behind-stage-presence.

BIBLIOGRAPHY

Westover, Jonathan H. "The Power of Storytelling: How Our Brains Are Wired for Narratives." *Human Capital Innovations*, January 11, 2024. https://www.innovativehumancapital.com/article/the-power-of-storytelling-how-our-brains-are-wired-for-narratives.

Wilson, Jamal. "Whooping: The Black Preaching Style That Wails, Shouts, and Sings the Sermon." *CNN*, October 20, 2010. https://www.cnn.com/2010/LIVING/10/20/whooping/index.html.

4: Resilience—*A Balm for the Burden*

American Psychological Association. "Building Your Resilience." Updated February 1, 2020. https://www.apa.org/topics/resilience/building-your-resilience.

Barna Group. "Most Black Adults Say Religion & the Black Experience Go Hand in Hand." February 18, 2021. www.barna.com/research/sobc-2/.

Cherry, Kendra. "Carol Dweck Biography (1956–)." *Explore Psychology*, updated March 6, 2023. https://www.explorepsychology.com/carol-dweck-biography/.

Duckworth, Angela. *Grit: The Power of Passion and Perseverance*. Scribner, 2016.

Hamilton, Jill B., Margarete Sandelowski, Angelo D. Moore, Mansi Agarwal, and Harold G. Koenig. "'You Need a Song to Bring You Through': The Use of Religious Songs to Manage Stressful Life Events." *Gerontologist* 53, no. 1 (2013): 26–38. https://doi.org/10.1093/geront/gns064.

Stych, Anne. "Understanding the Black Church Is Key to Appreciating the African American Experience, Study Says." *MinistryWatch*, February 23, 2021. https://ministrywatch.com/understanding-the-black-church-is-key-to-appreciating-the-african-american-experience-study-says/.

Taylor, Herman A., Jr., Tulani Washington-Plaskett, and Arshed A. Quyyumi. "Black Resilience: Broadening the Narrative and the Science on Cardiovascular Health and Disease Disparities." *Ethnicity and Disease* 30, no. 2 (2020): 365–68. https://www.ncbi.nlm.nih.gov/pmc/articles/PMC7186053/.

5: Perseverance—*Learning to Keep on Keeping On*

Abramson, Ashley. "Hope as the Antidote." *American Psychological Association Monitor* 55, no. 1 (2024): 88. https://www.apa.org/monitor/2024/01/trends-hope-greater-meaning-life.

BIBLIOGRAPHY

Bergland, Christopher. "The Neuroscience of Perseverance." *Psychology Today*, December 26, 2011. https://www.psychologytoday.com/intl/blog/the-athletes-way/201112/the-neuroscience-perseverance.

Chisholm, Shirley. "The Black Woman in Contemporary America." Speech, University of Missouri, Kansas City, June 17, 1974. *American RadioWorks*. https://americanradioworks.publicradio.org/features/blackspeech/schisholm.html.

Harris, Kamala. *Remarks by Vice President Harris at a Church Service | Greenville, NC*. The White House, October 13, 2024. https://bidenwhitehouse.archives.gov/briefing-room/speeches-remarks/2024/10/13/remarks-by-vice-president-harris-at-a-church-service-greenville-nc/.

Jackson, Jesse L. "1984 Democratic National Convention Speech." *Frontline*, PBS, July 18, 1984. https://www.pbs.org/wgbh/pages/frontline/jesse/speeches/jesse84speech.html.

Lunin, Monica. "Barack Obama Speech (The Audacity of Hope)." Mojologic, accessed May 25, 2025. https://www.mojologic.com.au/speech-14-barack-obama-the-audacity-of-hope/.

Obama, Barack. "A More Perfect Union." Speech, March 18, 2008. https://obamaspeeches.com/002-A-More-Perfect-Union-Obama-Speech.htm.

Penningroth, Dylan C. "Lessons from Martin Luther King Jr.'s Fight to Mobilize the Black Church." *Time*, January 13, 2024. https://time.com/6554880/martin-luther-king-jr-mobilize-black-church-essay/.

Sands, Darren. "Kamala Harris and Faith: A Baptist with a Jewish Spouse and Ties to the Black Church and Gandhi." *PBS News*, July 25, 2024. https://www.pbs.org/newshour/politics/kamala-harris-and-faith-a-baptist-with-a-jewish-spouse-and-ties-to-the-black-church-and-gandhi.

Shelton, Jason E. "The Black Church and the 2024 Presidential Election." Brookings Institution, May 15, 2024. https://www.brookings.edu/articles/the-black-church-and-the-2024-presidential-election/.

Shelton, Jason E., *The Contemporary Black Church: The New Dynamics of African American Religion*, New York University Press, 2024.

"Snyder's Hope Theory." *Mindtools*, accessed May 22, 2025. https://www.mindtools.com/aov3izj/snyders-hope-theory.

Sutton, Jeremy. "Martin Seligman's Positive Psychology Theory." PositivePsychology.com, October 4, 2016. https://positivepsychology.com/positive-psychology-theory.

Sutton, Jeremy. "The Role of Hope and Anticipation in Our Mental Wellbeing." *Positive Living Skills*, September 13, 2023. www.positivelivingskills.com.au/post/the-role-of-hope-and-anticipation-in-our-mental-wellbeing.

BIBLIOGRAPHY

Weems, Lovett H., Jr. "Shirley Chisholm's Applied Christianity." Lewis Center for Church Leadership, Wesley Theological Seminary, April 9, 2024. www.churchleadership.com/leading-ideas/shirley-chisholms-applied-christianity/.

Wellspan. "The Power of Anticipation: Why It Boosts Our Mental Health." May 24, 2024. https://www.wellspan.org/articles/2024/05/anticipation–mental-health-month-story.

6: Collaboration—*Leadership in a Song*

Amdal, Maren. "The Essential Role of Choir in Building Community." *Chorus Connection*, March 14, 2024. https://blog.chorusconnection.com/the-essential-role-of-choir-in-building-community.

Choir On. "The Importance of Choir Practice in the Church Community." June 3, 2024. https://choiron.com/blogs/news/the-importance-of-choir-practice-in-the-church-community.

Choir On. "The Life-Changing Spiritual Influence of Being in a Church Choir." March 18, 2024. https://choiron.com/blogs/news/the-life-changing-spiritual-influence-of-being-in-a-church-choir.

Claydon, Sarah. "The Science Behind Why Choir-Singing Is Good for You." CBC Radio, March 29, 2018. https://www.cbc.ca/radio/blogs/the-science-behind-why-choir-singing-is-good-for-you-1.4594292.

Common Ground. "Model for Local Church Collaboration." November 18, 2019. http://www.commongroundbeaverton.com/model-for-local-church-collaboration.

Gates, Henry Louis, Jr. *The Black Church: This Is Our Story, This Is Our Song*. Penguin Press, 2021.

"The Importance of Choir Practice in the Church Community." *Choir On*, June 3, 2024. https://choiron.com/blogs/news/the-importance-of-choir-practice-in-the-church-community.

Launay, Jacques, and Eiluned Pearce. "The New Science of Singing Together." *Greater Good Magazine*, December 4, 2015. https://greatergood.berkeley.edu/article/item/science_of_singing.

"The Life-Changing Spiritual Influence of Being in a Church Choir." *Choir On*, March 18, 2024. https://choiron.com/blogs/news/the-life-changing-spiritual-influence-of-being-in-a-church-choir.

National Park Service. "The Superpower of Singing: Music and the Struggle Against Slavery." Accessed May 22, 2025. https://www.nps.gov/articles/000/the-superpower-of-singing-music-and-the-struggle-against-slavery.htm.

Quito, Anne. "What Choral Singing Can Teach Us About Leadership." *Quartz*, December 12, 2018. https://qz.com/work/1491154/what-chorale-singing-can-teach-us-about-leadership.

Scheidhauer, Laura. "3 Essentials for Teambuilding—Lessons I Learned from the Choir." LinkedIn. April 16, 2020. https://www.linkedin.com/pulse/3-essentials-teambuilding-lessons-i-learned-from-laura-scheidhauer/.

Sutton, Jeremy. "Martin Seligman's Positive Psychology Theory." PositivePsychology.com, October 4, 2016. https://positivepsychology.com/positive-psychology-theory/.

Taylor, W. David O. "Hymns and Neurons: How Worship Rewires Our Brains and Bonds Us Together." *Christianity Today*, August 29, 2022. https://www.christianitytoday.com/2022/08/worship-church-music-hymns-brains-bond-together/.

7: Accountability—*Keeping It Righteous*

Bartel, Jeffrey. "Creating a Culture of Accountability and Responsibility." *Forbes*, July 30, 2024. www.forbes.com/councils/forbesfinancecouncil/2024/07/30/creating-a-culture-of-accountability-and-responsibility/.

Cantero-Gomez, Paloma. "The 5 Rules Followed by Accountable Leaders." *Forbes*, June 7, 2019. www.forbes.com/sites/palomacanterogomez/2019/06/07/the-5-rules-followed-by-accountable-leaders/.

Di Domenico, Stefano I., and Richard M. Ryan. "The Emerging Neuroscience of Intrinsic Motivation: A New Frontier in Self-Determination Research." *Frontiers in Human Neuroscience* 11 (2017). doi:10.3389/fnhum.2017.00145.

Fouts, Melinda. "How to Enhance Company Culture Using Accountability." *Forbes*, July 11, 2024. www.forbes.com/councils/forbescoachescouncil/2024/07/11/how-to-enhance-company-culture-using-accountability/.

Henzel, David. "What Is Personal Accountability: How to Hold Yourself Responsible." Love Not Fear. Accessed May 22, 2025. https://lovenotfear.com/personal-behaviour/personal-accountability/.

Jeremiah. "Intrinsic vs. Extrinsic Motivation: What Drives Us Forward." *GoalsWon Blog*, July 23, 2024. https://www.goalswon.com/blog/intrinsic-vs-extrinsic-motivation-how-to-align-ourselves-with-what-drives-us-forward.

Li, Meng, and Timothy A. Judge. "Leadership, Justice, and the Importance of Voice." *Lead Read Today*, December 3, 2019. https://fisher.osu.edu/blogs/leadreadtoday/blog/leadership-justice-and-the-importance-of-voice.

Stobierski, Tim. "5 Pros and Cons of Authoritative Leadership." Harvard Business School Online, November 12, 2019. https://online.hbs.edu/blog/post/authoritative-leadership-style.

US Office of Personnel Management. "Accountability Can Have Positive Results." Performance Management. Accessed May 22, 2025. https://www.opm.gov/policy-data-oversight/performance-management/reference-materials/more-topics/accountability-can-have-positive-results/.

Witvliet, Charlotte V.O., Sung Joon Jang, Byron R. Johnson, C. Stephen Evans, Jack W. Berry, Joseph Leman, Robert C. Roberts, John Peteet, Andrew B. Torrance, and Ashley N. Hayden. "Accountability: Construct Definition and Measurement of a Virtue Vital to Flourishing." *Journal of Positive Psychology* 18, no 5 (2023): 660–63. https://doi.org/10.1080/17439760.2022.2109203.

8: Social Justice—*A Legacy of Overcoming*

American Committee for the Weizmann Institute of Science. "Brave Brains: Neural Mechanisms of Courage." Accessed May 22, 2025. https://www.weizmann-usa.org/news-media/in-the-news/brave-brains-neural-mechanisms-of-courage/.

CBS News. "Black Church Divided on Obama, Wright." April 29, 2008. www.cbsnews.com/news/black-church-divided-on-obama-wright/.

FiveThirtyEight. "Obama and the Rev. Wright Controversy: What Really Happened?" Accessed May 22, 2025. https://fivethirtyeight.com/videos/obama-and-the-rev-wright-controversy-what-really-happened/.

Goldstein-Gelb, Warren. "The B-Change Podcast: Exploring the Intersection of Positive Psychology and Social Justice." Wholebeing Institute, accessed May 22, 2025. https://wholebeinginstitute.com/b-change-podcast-positive-psychology-social-justice/.

Harvey, Robert S. "Restoring the Social Justice Identity of the Black Church." *Inquiries Journal* 2, no. 2 (2010). https://www.inquiriesjournal.com/articles/162/restoring-the-social-justice-identity-of-the-black-church.

Heim, Christian. "How Does Courage Work in Your Brain?" Dr. Christian Heim, April 17, 2024. https://www.drchristianheim.com/blog/2024/4/17/how-does-courage-work-in-your-brain.

Henderson, Stephen. *American Black Journal with Stephen Henderson*. Season 51, episode 30, "The Power of the Prophetic Voice in the Black Church." Aired July 25, 2023, on PBS. www.pbs.org/video/the-power-of-the-prophetic-voice-in-the-black-church-vftky9/.

Interaction Consulting Group. "The Neuroscience of Courage." LinkedIn, March 14, 2024. https://www.linkedin.com/pulse/neuroscience-courage-interaction-consulting-group-6flqc/.

McGrady, Clyde. "The Black Church Has a Gen-Z Issue: 'They Don't Come Into the Building Anymore.'" New York Times, September 29, 2024. https://www.nytimes.com/2024/09/29/us/politics/black-church-gen-z-attendance.html.

Montagne, Renee, and Juan Williams. "Analysis: Rev. Wright's Comments on Black Church." NPR, April 29, 2008. www.npr.org/2008/04/29/90024842/analysis-rev-wrights-comments-on-black-church.

Mount Sinai School of Medicine. "Researchers Identify Area of the Brain That Processes Empathy." September 1, 2012. www.mountsinai.org/about/newsroom/2012/researchers-identify-area-of-the-brain-that-processes-empathy.

Obama, Barack. "A More Perfect Union." Speech, March 18, 2008. Accessed May 22, 2025. https://obamaspeeches.com/002-A-More-Perfect-Union-Obama-Speech.htm.

"Perspectives: Jeremiah Wright and the Black Church." Religion & Ethics Newsweekly, May 2, 2008. www.pbs.org/wnet/religionandethics/2008/05/02/perspectives-jeremiah-wright-and-the-black-church/76/.

Sedarati, Bahar. "Rewiring the Brain for Bravery." LinkedIn, March 26, 2023. https://www.linkedin.com/pulse/rewiring-brain-bravery-bahar-sedarati-md-cpe-fcucm-/.

Volz, Brian D. "Race and Quarterback Survival in the National Football League." Journal of Sports Economics 18, no. 8 (2017): 765–92. https://doi.org/10.1177/1527002515609659.

Wright, Jeremiah. "Jeremiah Wright Interview: The Controversial Sermon's Impact on Obama's Campaign." Posted October 28, 2021 by Life Stories. YouTube, 54:32. http://youtube.com/watch?v=irv3ev9j8Wg.

Yoder, Keith J., and Jean Decety. "The Neuroscience of Morality and Social Decision-Making." Psychology, Crime & Law 24, no. 3 (2017): 279–95. https://pmc.ncbi.nlm.nih.gov/articles/PMC6372234/.

Zeleny, Jeff, and Adam Nagourney. "An Angry Obama Renounces Ties to His Ex-Pastor." New York Times, April 30, 2008. https://www.nytimes.com/2008/04/30/us/politics/30obama.html.

9: Creativity and Innovation—*Miracles and Blessings*

Agbor, Emmanuel. "Creativity and Innovation: The Leadership Dynamics." Journal of Strategic Leadership 1, no. 1 (2008). https://www.regent.edu/journal/journal-of-strategic-leadership/creativity-and-innovation-the-leadership-dynamics.

Aurora Training Advantage. "Creativity: A Key Trait of an Effective Leader." Accessed May 22, 2025. https://auroratrainingadvantage.com/leadership/creativity-key-trait-effective-leader/.

Aurora Training Advantage. "Creative Problem-Defined." Accessed May 22, 2025. https://auroratrainingadvantage.com/leadership/key-term/creative-problem-solving/.

Copley, Laura. "Discovering Self-Empowerment: 13 Methods to Foster It." PositivePsychology.com, February 21, 2024. https://positivepsychology.com/self-empowerment/.

Decety, Jean, and Keith J. Yoder. "Empathy and Motivation for Justice: Cognitive Empathy and Concern, but Not Emotional Empathy, Predict Sensitivity to Injustice for Others." *Social Neuroscience* 11, no. 1 (2015): 1–14. https://pmc.ncbi.nlm.nih.gov/articles/PMC4592359/.

Frederickson, Barbara. "The Role of Positive Emotions in Positive Psychology." *American Psychologist* 56, no. 3 (2001): 218–26.

"Innovative Thinking: Fostering Creativity in Leadership." *Arti Halai*, March 27, 2024. https://www.artihalai.com/innovative-thinking-fostering-creativity-in-leadership/.

ITD World. "Creative Leadership." *ITD World Blog*, accessed May 22, 2025. https://itdworld.com/blog/leadership/creative-leadership/.

"Leadership and Innovation: Fostering a Culture of Creativity." *Economic Times*, October 17, 2023. https://m.economictimes.com/jobs/leadership-and-innovation-fostering-a-culture-of-creativity/articleshow/104630477.cms.

Makice, Amy. "Neuroscience for Connection." Bloomington Center for Connection, January 9, 2025. www.bloomingtoncenterforconnection.org/2025/01/neuroscience-for-connection/.

The Neuroscience School. "The Neuroscience School." Accessed May 22, 2025. https://neuroscienceschool.com/.

Wilner, Joe. "The Top 10 Positive Emotions." *Psych Central*, March 15, 2011. https://psychcentral.com/blog/positive-psychology/2011/03/the-top-10-positive-emotions#1.

10: Economic Empowerment—*Building Kingdoms*

BillMari. "The Black Church: Key to Black Economic Empowerment." *Medium*, May 17, 2018. https://medium.com/@iloveblackpeopleapp/the-black-church-key-to-black-economic-empowerment-64bccca499b8.

"Can Churches Fix America's Affordable-Housing Crunch?" *The Economist*, republished by *Enterprise Community Partners*, August 8, 2024. https://www.economist.com/united-states/2024/08/08/can-churches-fix-americas-affordable-housing-crunch.

BIBLIOGRAPHY

Connelly, Christopher. "This Dallas Church Acquired a Bank to Offer an Alternative to Payday Loans." *KERA News*, March 30, 2021. www.keranews.org/news/2021-03-30/this-dallas-church-acquired-a-bank-to-offer-an-alternative-to-payday-loans.

Copley, Laura. "Discovering Self-Empowerment: 13 Methods to Foster It." PositivePsychology.com, February 21, 2024. https://positivepsychology.com/self-empowerment/.

Faulks, Baira, Yinghua Song, Moses Wainganjo, Bojan Obrenovic, and Danijela Dohinic. "Impact of Empowering Leadership, Innovative Work, and Organizational Learning Readiness on Sustainable Economic Performance: An Empirical Study of Companies in Russia during the COVID-19 Pandemic." *Sustainability* 13, no. 22 (2021). https://doi.org/10.3390/su132212465.

Gardiner, Kirsty. "Psychological Safety and Positive Psychology: A Leadership Guide." PositivePsychology.com, September 21, 2023. https://positivepsychology.com/psychological-safety/.

Gleeson, Brent. "The Empowerment Imperative: Unlocking Leadership's Greatest Advantage." *Forbes*, January 10, 2025. https://www.forbes.com/sites/brentgleeson/2025/01/10/the-empowerment-imperative-unlocking-leaderships-greatest-advantage/.

Good Street Baptist Church. "History." Accessed May 22, 2025. https://www.goodstreetbaptistchurch.org/history.

Harris, Carla. "GLS18 Session Notes—Carla Harris: Characteristics of a L.E.A.D.E.R." Global Leadership Network, accessed May 22, 2025. https://globalleadership.org/articles/leading-others/gls18-session-notes-carla-harris-characteristics-of-a-l-e-a-d-e-r/.

Makice, Amy. "Neuroscience for Connection." Bloomington Center for Connection, January 9, 2025. https://www.bloomingtoncenterforconnection.org/2025/01/neuroscience-for-connection/.

"Millermore Mansion in Dallas." City-Data, accessed May 22, 2025. www.city-data.com/articles/Millermore-Mansion-in-Dallas.html.

Mitchell, Deah Berry. "Dinner on the Ground: The History of Sunday Feasts at Black Churches in Dallas and Beyond." *Dallas Morning News*, September 17, 2021. https://www.dallasnews.com/food/cooking/2021/09/17/dinner-on-the-ground-the-history-of-sunday-feasts-at-black-churches-in-dallas-and-beyond.

PositivePsychology.com. "Empowering and Inspiring Others Through Positive Leadership." LinkedIn, November 3, 2023. https://www.linkedin.com/pulse/empowering-inspiring-others-through-positive-snrqe/.

Stobierski, Tim. "5 Pros & Cons of Authoritative Leadership." Harvard Business School Online, November 12, 2019. https://online.hbs.edu/blog/post/authoritative-leadership-style.

UN Women. "Facts and Figures: Economic Empowerment." Updated February 2024. https://www.unwomen.org/en/what-we-do/economic-empowerment/facts-and-figures.

"Wells Fargo and T. D. Jakes Group Announce Ten-Year Strategic Partnership to Build Inclusive Communities." Wells Fargo Newsroom, April 27, 2023. https://stories.wf.com/newsroom/wells-fargo-and-td-jakes-group-announce-ten-year-strategic-partnership.

Wooldridge, Leslie Quander, and Kit Pulliam. "36 Black-Owned Banks and Credit Unions, Sorted by State." *Business Insider*, December 31, 2024. https://www.businessinsider.com/personal-finance/black-owned-banks-credit-unions.

General Citations

Evans, Tony. *A Survey of The Black Church in America*. Harvest House Publishers, 2021.

Mellowes, Marilyn. "The Black Church." *American Experience*, accessed May 22, 2025. https://www.pbs.org/wgbh/americanexperience/features/godinamerica-black-church.

Penningroth, Dylan C. "Lessons from Martin Luther King Jr.'s Fight to Mobilize the Black Church." *TIME*, January 13, 2024. https://time.com/6554880/martin-luther-king-jr-mobilize-black-church-essay/.

Stych, Anne. "Understanding the Black Church Is Key to Appreciating the African American Experience, Study Says." MinistryWatch, February 23, 2021. https://ministrywatch.com/understanding-the-black-church-is-key-to-appreciating-the-african-american-experience-study-says/.

Suarez, Cyndi. "The Perils of Black Leadership." *Nonprofit Quarterly*, May 15, 2023. https://nonprofitquarterly.org/the-perils-of-black-leadership/.

About the Author

L. MICHELLE SMITH is the premiere voice in leadership at the apex of science and culture. She changes organizations for the better by transforming the lives and leadership of executives within them. Seen on local, national, and international media outlets, she is a bestselling and award-winning author, Fortune 100 C-Suite adviser, ICF-certified global executive, and life coach and the CEO/founder of no silos communications llc. NSC is a media and consulting company that develops high-performing executive leaders with a specialty in women and women of color. Positive psychology and neuroscience informed and credentialed by the International Coaching Federation, she runs an international coaching and consulting practice where she works with professionals and organizations to create learning and coaching experiences that inspire exceptional lives and leadership. A certified DiSC practitioner, she is also an adjunct faculty member of the Executive Leadership Council Institute and a faculty member for the Coaching and Applied Positive Psychology Institute. She is the EP, creator, and host of the global show *The Culture Soup Podcast*® and her leadership podcast on Substack *Her Next Power Move*. A highly regarded speaker and facilitator, she is also a contributor for *HuffPost* "Voices."